IMPAIRED BODIES, GENDERED LIVES
EVERYDAY REALITIES OF DISABLED WOMEN

IMPAIRED BODIES, GENDERED LIVES

Everyday Realities of Disabled Women

NANDINI GHOSH

PRIMUS BOOKS

PRIMUS BOOKS
An imprint of Ratna Sagar P. Ltd.
Virat Bhavan
Mukherjee Nagar Commercial Complex
Delhi 110 009

Offices at CHENNAI LUCKNOW
AGRA AHMEDABAD BENGALURU COIMBATORE DEHRADUN GUWAHATI
HYDERABAD JAIPUR JALANDHAR KANPUR KOCHI KOLKATA MADURAI
MUMBAI PATNA RANCHI VARANASI

First published 2016

ISBN: 978-93-84082-50-5 (Hardback)
ISBN: 978-93-84092-26-9 (POD)
ISBN: 978-93-84092-27-6 (e-book)

Published by Primus Books

Lasertypeset by Sai Graphic Design
Arakashan Road, Paharganj, New Delhi 110 055

Printed and bound in India by Replika Press Pvt. Ltd.

Contents

Acknowledgements

This book is the culmination of academic explorations in the arena of gender and disability based on my grassroots-level field experiences of working with persons with disabilities in West Bengal and Jharkhand. I have been associated with NGOs in West Bengal, Jharkhand and Odisha working on issues of disability and community-based rehabilitation as well as involved in disability activism with rights groups in India. Inspiration for taking up, continuing and completing this research was provided by many people, some of whom I seek to acknowledge here.

At the onset, I would like to recognize the influence of late Jane Webb and Marcette Buttigieg, my mentors in the field of disability and who have been working tirelessly for disabled people in the eastern regions of India. The other major stimulus was provided by Professor Padma Velaskar of Tata Institute of Social Sciences, who focused my attention on the minutest details and the most critical issues, and helped to conceptualize and give shape to the study in a holistic way.

I wish to thank the Jawaharlal Nehru Memorial Fund for sponsoring my study from 2004–6 and giving me the status of a Nehru Memorial Fellow. I would also like to express my gratitude to the help and support received from different libraries—National Library, Centre for Studies in Social Sciences library, Jadavpur University Women's Studies library, Institute of Development Studies Kolkata library, Jawaharlal Nehru University library, Centre for Women's Development Studies library in New Delhi, Banaras Hindu University library in Varanasi, Shreemati Nathibai Damodar Thackersey Women's University's (SNDT) Women's Studies library in Mumbai and the British Council and American Centre libraries in India; and discussions I had with Tom Shakespeare and Geraldine Forbes in Mumbai and Anita Ghai in New Delhi, and other discussions with different people in related fields of study. I wish to thank the staff of the NGOs through which I set up contact with some of the women participating in this study, for helping me finding the women, for making my stay with them easier, escorting me on initial visits to the villages, and answering my umpteen queries painstakingly.

I would also like to acknowledge the role of my parents who have been a guiding force in all the things that I have done in my life. Their unstinting support and encouragement in all that I have attempted, the values that they have given me and the lessons that I have learnt from them will forever inspire me to aspire towards greater heights not only professionally but also towards being a better human being.

I would also like to express my appreciation of the strength, courage and zest for life of all the women with disabilities who participated in this study and thank them and their families for welcoming my intrusion into their lives, my questions and interactions, both of which enriched my life and knowledge. Their friendship now enriches my life and assures me of an extended family in different areas of Kolkata and South 24 Parganas. I would also like to mention specially the passing away of Dora, one of my friends and participants in this study, during the course of my data analysis, whose voice resonates through this study with all the aspirations, hopes, wishes, dreams, fears, and stigma encountered and grappled with by most disabled women.

Kolkata NANDINI GHOSH

CHAPTER I

Introduction

'Disability' is a complex category. It has always been understood and interpreted by different people in very different ways. Historically, all societies have assumed that individuals with physical or intellectual anomalies are, by the very nature of their condition, inferior. The connotation of lack or deficiency associated with any form of mental, physical or sensory disability has been universal over time and space. However, it has to be acknowledged that the word 'disability' is itself not a homogeneous category, subsuming under it different kinds of bodily variations, physical impairments, sensory deficits and mental or learning inadequacies, which may be either congenital or acquired.

My interest in researching the lives of disabled women took root in my childhood years when 'being different' took root in my deepest consciousness. All through my growing up years, I was constantly subjected to pointed fingers, stares and suppressed laughter whenever I was in the public arena. It was only when I started working in the field of disability after completing my higher education that I realized that I had been struggling against the disability identity which was thrust upon me by the people around me. Although I didn't seem to 'bother' my friends and family, I was made to be aware of and also accept the fact that I was 'different'. It all led to a great devaluation of my sense of self.

After exploring the broad arena of disability studies, I am now better able to understand the relevance of the social model in the lives of people with disabilities. I also recognize now that I too had been struggling against an oppressive society that establishes a norm or standard, judging people against it and labelling them as different or disabled. As neither my family nor I ever thought of myself as different/disabled, my life experiences were similar to those of most people my age—going to school, participating in family and social functions, going out with friends, and socialization within the family. My so-called impairments never restricted my life in any way.

My interest in the field of Disability Studies took a firmer root during my field level engagement with different rehabilitation programmes being run in the mid-1990s for persons with disabilities. The major part of the work in disability in India has been at the level of practice—government and non-government agencies working for the rehabilitation of disabled people, providing services that are mostly institutional and some which were community based. There are advantages and disadvantages to both these approaches. Institutional services are highly developed and use sophisticated techniques in controlled contexts to maximize the development potential of the child or person with the disability. However, these institutional services are expensive and available mostly in urban areas, making them mostly inaccessible for the majority of people living in rural areas. Community-based work is both time and energy intensive, and changes are visible only after prolonged periods of interventions. However, there was little effort made to study disabled people within their socio-cultural and economic contexts and to understand the experience of disablement from the perspective of the disabled person. The thrust remained on normalization through medical or therapeutic interventions to enable disabled people to function as 'normally' as possible in society. The onus was on the disabled person to modify and adjust his/her 'special' needs to the existing physical and social environment.

Invisibility is imposed on people with disabilities, through ideas about their incapability and reduced capacities, hostile physical and social arrangements, and insensitive and exclusionary institutional set-ups. People with disabilities face a range of challenges, from dealing with personal experiences of impairment to negative attitudes of family and kinfolk, and discriminatory social structures and from institutional systems like schools, hospitals and work spheres. While their families accept and love them, they are visibly relegated to the margins because of the socio-cultural and political ideologies. There is also a distinct gender bias in the seeking of rehabilitation services. Most of those who came to the rehabilitation centres were boys. The few girls who came were very young (between 6 and 10 years). Perhaps this was so because parents hoped that by the time she entered her teens, their daughter would be able to lead a 'normal' life. I realized that complex social processes that impinge upon the lives of these disabled girls, determine the ways in which they interpret and give meaning to their daily existence.

My exploration into the lives and experiences of disabled people to reveal the complexity of their situation in their families and communities also brought the realization that the word 'disability' is an umbrella term spanning a range of impairments, and affecting individuals differently, depending upon other factors in their environments and in their own lives. One method of comprehending the systems prevalent in any society is by exploring the state policies that reflect the attitude towards people with disabilities.

Disability Discourse in India

According to the Census 2011, there are 26,810,557 disabled people in India, of which women with disabilities constitute 44.1 per cent. The data reveals that of the five categories of disabilities on which data has been collected, people with locomotor impairments constitute the bulk of the disabled population (20.3 per cent), followed by people with speech and hearing impairments (18.9 per cent) and people with visual impairments (18.8 per cent). People with multiple disabilities (7.9 per cent) and mental retardation (5.6 per cent) along with other disabilities (18.9 per cent) comprise almost rest of the disabled population. In India, the state has always assumed responsibility for providing the welfare of disabled citizens. Thus, in historical texts,[1] there are references to residential institutions and hospitals for the physically disabled (that included the blind, crippled and deaf people) and the infirm (Mani 1988). In the colonial period, institutions for disabled people were set up mainly in towns with religious shrines (like Varanasi and Lucknow), where there was a preponderance of disabled people living off the charity of visiting pilgrims. These schools and residential institutions founded by nineteenth-century reformers aimed at providing education and vocational training to disabled people, mainly the visually and orthopaedically impaired. There were also sporadic efforts to set up hospitals and charitable institutions by individual philanthropists, especially after World War II. But the problems of disabled people were not addressed in a comprehensive manner (ibid.). However, an important step for providing accurate information towards guiding policy for the disabled was taken at the initiative of the colonial rulers: from the first census in India in 1872 to all the subsequent ones till 1931, data about different categories of disabled people (physically and intellectually disabled and also a leprosy affected) was collected.

While there was no clear-cut policy during colonial rule and even after independence, the general attitude towards the disabled has been one of charity and welfare. After independence, the state in India accepted social welfare as a state responsibility, seeking to promote the welfare of the weaker sections of society, defined as groups of individuals in need of special considerations like children, women, people from certain Scheduled Castes and Tribes, and disabled people. Thus, welfare activities that had been the responsibility of voluntary or religious organizations now became state responsibility (Billimoria 1985). The Constitution of India has guaranteed through the Directive Principles of State Policy and Fundamental Rights, equality before the law and equal protection of law for all its citizens, and prohibited discrimination on the grounds of 'religion, race, caste, sex, place of birth'. However, the orientation towards people with disabilities has been that of welfare, as is evident from Article 41 which stipulates: 'The state shall, within the limits of its economic capacity and development make effective provision for securing the right to work, to education and to public assistance in cases of unemployment, old age, sickness and disablement' (Pandey and Advani 1995).

The reluctance of the government in formulating and implementing a coherent disability policy reflects the socio-cultural assumptions about the disabled in India, where a religio-moral-medical model of disability still prevails. The socio-religious conceptualization of disability is that impairment is divine retribution for past or present sins, and disabled people are looked upon as objects of pity. While the welfare approach towards other disadvantaged sections of the population like women, children and the Scheduled Castes/Tribes led to comprehensive state-initiated policies and programmes, the attitude towards disabled people has been only one of token inclusion and a general neglect and apathy for their concerns. The state, influenced by medical professionals and notions of normalization, concentrated on providing facilities for medical treatment and management of people with different orthopaedic and sensory disabilities, like restorative surgery, provision for assistive aids and appliances and different therapeutic interventions along with scholarships and aid for special schools in the field of education (Mohit and Rungta 2000).

The welfare state in India with its emphasis on both charity as well as on medical aspects of rehabilitation lacked the political will to encourage the empowerment of disabled people. There was little direct commitment towards bringing about changes at the social or political levels. The individualistic orientation of the programmes towards the disabled people is also evident from the fact that other important concerns like integration, social attitudes, access, etc., received little attention as the aim was to secure the welfare of the disabled individual, without intervening at the level of community practices.

The apathy of the state in developing a comprehensive policy for persons with disabilities becomes apparent from its sporadic efforts, initially in 1970–1 and then in 1980, to draft a suitable law for the disabled. These half-hearted strategies, however, were initiated only due to the pressure from international developments, like the United Nations General Assembly's Declaration on the Rights of the Disabled Persons in 1975, and the declaration of 1981 as the International Year for Disabled Persons. In the international sphere, disability came to be recognized as a human rights issue, and in 1985 the Universal Declaration of Human Rights was specifically extended to include disabled people (Priestley 2001). The International Decade of Disabled Persons (1983–92) culminated in the development of United Nations Rules on the Equalization of Opportunities for Disabled Persons in 1993. In Asia too, the Economic and Social Commission of Asia and the Pacific (ESCAP) declared 1993–2002 as the Asia and the Pacific Decade of Disabled Persons to give impetus to the implementation of the World Programme of Action in the ESCAP region.[2] In response to such international developments and increasing pressure from disability activists in India, the Government of India enacted the Persons with Disabilities (Equal Opportunities, Protection of Rights and Full Participation) Act in 1995. However, the law came into force only in February 1996 (Mohit 2000).

The hurried passage of the Persons with Disabilities Act in India in 1995, forestalled the drafting of a comprehensive policy which would include a broader set of initiatives, decisions, priorities or guidelines that address a goal and a plan for its achievement. This Act, thus, became the first policy statement in India which recognized the rights of people with various impairments to equal opportunity in participating fully in social, cultural, economic, and educational programmes of the country. The National Policy for Persons with Disabilities in India, which came into effect in 2006, is a more forward-looking document because of the influence of the United Nations Convention on the Rights of Persons with Disabilities, which was passed in 2007 and became an international law in 2008. The National Policy for Persons with Disability 2006 attempts to clarify the framework under which the state, civil society and private sector must operate in order to ensure a dignified life for persons with disability and support for their caregivers. The policy recognizes the need to replace the earlier emphasis on *medical rehabilitation* with an emphasis on *social rehabilitation*. Community Based Rehabilitation (CBR) is seen as an effective means of rehabilitation, and the policy states that CBR will be encouraged.

Although the National Policy (2005) 'recognizes that Persons with Disabilities are a valuable human resource for the country and seeks to create an environment that provides them equal opportunities, protection of their rights and full participation in society', it limits itself to only reiterating the provisions enlisted in the different laws for persons with disabilities in India. The Persons with Disabilities Act 1995 has defined disability in strictly medical terms, proceeding from the medical model of disability that ignores the social perceptions about disability (Mohit and Rungta 2000). Thus, the categories of disability, blindness and low vision, leprosy cured who have lost limbs or have lost functional ability, hearing impairment, locomotor disability, mental retardation, and mental illness are all dependent on certification by medical professionals. This highlights and legitimizes the control of the medical professionals over the diagnosis, management and interventions for the disabled. This does not take into account that many disabilities are conditions that may not need medical interventions or management, but a more inclusive attitude towards the disabled person and his/her needs. The Act has, however, left out some groups—people with epilepsy, older people with disabilities and certain genetic conditions as well as learning disabilities and attention disorders—which can be very disabling in different social setups.

The main thrust of the Act has been to spell out the state's responsibility towards prevention of impairments and protection of disabled people's rights in health, education, training, employment, and rehabilitation. The Act treats disability as a civil right, and lays down provisions for creating a barrier-free environment for disabled people as well as removing discrimination and abuse against them. There are extensive strategies laid down for development of comprehensive programmes and services for equalization of opportunities for disabled people in the sphere of education and employment and provisions for the integration of disabled people into mainstream society. The Act also emphasized the need for supporting institutions for persons with disabilities as well as social security provisions for the disabled (Pandey and Advani 1995; Mohit and Rungta 2000). In spite of focusing on different aspects of the lives of disabled people, the Act has sustained its inclination towards the medical model of disability, by projecting disability as an individual problem that can be remedied through different interventions and specialized services. The Act has ignored the definitions of disability advocated by the social model, which lays more stress on the disabling barriers faced by people with impairments and press for structural changes within society.

Instituting Feminist Disability Studies in India

Disability activists and scholars in Western countries have been using the different models of disability to try to explain the changing social perceptions about disability and disabled people. While these models have been conceptually distinguished from one another, they coexist and interact in most communities, impinging considerably on the lives and experiences of disabled people. The individual model of disability primarily locates the 'problem' of disability within the individual, stemming from the functional limitations or psychological losses which are assumed to arise from disability (Campling 1983; Oliver 1990; Silvers, Wasserman and Mahowald 1998). However, the reasons for and impact of the disability may be explained by the socio-culturally and historically variable constructions about disabled people. These models include a range of views about disability, ranging from the religious/moral ideas about causes of disability, to considering it as a personal tragedy, to the administrative or welfare orientation towards disability. Disability, as a personal tragedy, considers that individuals diagnosed to be 'suffering' from a particular condition or impairment are 'helpless dependants, incapable of mastering the elementary skills essential for engaging in productive social and economic activities' (Thomas 1982; Lonsdale 1990). Thus, disability also carries with it the connotation of functional limitation and inability, as against familiar ways of functioning, magnifying 'normal' bodily and intellectual performances into standards that render disabled people incompetent and incapacitated. Being disabled, thus, entails a reduction in the opportunities for people with disabilities and also in their obligations (Silvers, Wasserman and Mahowald 1998). Disability, by virtue of the functional limitations it represents, is seen to alter people profoundly rendering them naturally unequal and in need of protection and welfare (ibid.). Critiquing the medical model because of its biologically deterministic stress on physical or sensory deficits, disability scholars have pointed to the fact that it ignores or denies the subjective social experiences that unite disabled people, and focuses only on the medical dimensions of difference (Shakespeare 1996). Abberley (1987) rejects normalizing philosophies that fail to locate abnormality in the society and assume abnormality to reside within the individual. Normalizing programmes, imposed to force anomalous individuals to adjust to environments that are suited to the dominant social classes, totally ignore the role of obstructive environments in creating 'dysfunctionality'. There is a denial of common social experiences which unite disabled people; the focus is only on the medical dimensions of difference (Shakespeare 1996).

Disability Studies emerged as an interdisciplinary and multidisciplinary field of study only by the end of the twentieth century, drawing on the insights of critical, race, gender, and queer theories. Disability Studies defines disability not as a physical deficit or defect inherent in certain bodies or brains, but rather as a relationship of differential power or privilege. This challenges the view of disability as an individual deficit or defect that can be remedied solely through medical intervention or rehabilitation by 'experts' and other service providers. Focusing on the disadvantage typically experienced by those who are disabled, primarily reflecting the way society defines and responds to certain types of 'difference', it explores models and theories that examine social, political, cultural, and economic factors that define disability and help determine personal and collective responses to difference. The social model recognizes that disability is not the outcome of bodily pathology but is socially produced by systematic patterns of exclusion that are built into the social fabric (Shakespeare 1994; Hughes and Paterson 1997). Drawing on the social model of disability, scholars of Disability Studies have reframed the concept of disability in terms of power relationships between the disabled and the non-disabled, based on the social and cultural interpretations of different impairments which lead to their marginalization and stigmatization. In all societies, the experience of disability is mediated by socio-cultural constructions that give meaning to impairments and influence the experiences and interactions of disabled people in different socio-historical contexts. The social interpretation and experience of such varied types of physical and mental impairments also differ depending on the socio-cultural contexts. These contexts influence the definitions and interpretations of various kinds of physical and mental inadequacies as well as the resources available to facilitate the inclusion of disabled people within the community.

Feminist Disability Studies begins with the assumption that disability is always inextricably linked to other social markers, such as gender, race, sexuality, and social class. Disabled feminist scholars in the late 1990s posited an alternate understanding of disabled women, a new framework that enables an exchange between disability theory and feminism, in order to understand how bodies—marked by gender and by disability, by impairment and sex—are formed in, created by, and acted upon by society, and also act within and impact society (Morris 1998; Schriempf 2001). The gendered approach to disability recognizes that disability has a profound impact on the lives of both disabled men and women in such a way that their lived experiences within different socio-cultural formations influence the ways in which they negotiate and develop strategies to counter the labels of incapability, weakness and dependence that are thrust on them by the able-bodied world. Socio-cultural ideologies and constructions of gender and disability greatly affect the perceptions of disabled people about themselves and influence their life experiences within their communities. Recognizing the fact that both disability and gender represent unequal power relationships, these theories stress that cultural representations of gender coupled with constructions of disability affect the real lived experiences of men and women with disabilities. The challenging of accepted cultural constructions of disability and gender has also led to a better understanding about the ways in which disabled people negotiate their gender identities in their daily lives. Thus, a gendered analysis of disability challenges cultural constructions of gender and disability. It also explores the different ways in which disabled men and women themselves experience, negotiate and subvert the gendering process. As physical impairment is inevitably associated with bodily deficits, this approach examines the role of the gendered body in structuring the experiences of disabled men and women in society. This exploratory study is ethnographic in nature and relies on qualitative techniques of data collection to reconstruct and understand the lives of disabled women in their own social contexts.

Doing Feminist Ethnography: Exploring the Lives of Disabled Women

Feminist epistemologies draw on critical and constructivist paradigms as well as historically situated and trustworthy empirical materials in order to make lived experience central to qualitative enquiry (Denzin and Lincoln 1998). Feminist standpoint epistemologies are concerned with portraying the lived realities of women's lives, acknowledging the fact that all attempts to know are socially situated. The social situation of an epistemic agent—her gender, class, race, ethnicity, sexuality, and physical capacities—plays a role in forming what we know and limiting what we are able to know. They can affect what we are capable of knowing and what we are permitted to know. The influence of social location on epistemic content and capacity can be felt throughout our epistemic practices, shaping not only the way in which we understand the world, but also the way in which it is presented to us via experience. Feminist researchers are, thus, seen as knowing subjects, producing knowledge of a real social world, in order to elaborate how gendered social life is organized, structured and made meaningful. This means producing new knowledge by reinterpreting experiences, emotions and meanings attached to behaviour within different normative frameworks that are grounded in how women voice their experiences.

Feminist research demands that the voices of women speak in and through the interpretive texts. Giving voice to women's perspectives means identifying ways in which women create meaning and experience life from their particular position in the social hierarchy. According to Smith (1987), feminist research must strive to create space for an absent subject, and an absent experience, with the presence and spoken experience of actual women speaking about their everyday worlds. Feminist research has always stressed the fact that knowledge must be grounded contextually in the concrete realm of women's everyday lives (Stacey 1988). Both ethnography and feminism thus have experience, participants, definitions, meanings and subjectivity, as a focus and always take the context into account. The aim is to map out the physical, cultural and economic possibilities for social action and meaning, understand the interaction between structure and agency and enable women participants to have some say in how they are studied.

Ethnographic research involves the utilization of different research techniques and is conducted within settings of the participants in order to gain an understanding of how the context informs the actions. It engages the researcher in participation and observation, involving an account of the development of relationships between the researcher and the researched over a prolonged period of time, and focusing on how experience and practice are a part of wider processes (Skeggs 2001). Willis (1981) articulates this as showing 'the cultural viewpoint of the oppressed, their hidden knowledges and resistances'. Feminist ethnography emphasizes that knowledge is contextual and interpersonal, based on women's experiences within the concrete realm of everyday reality and human agency. This feminist method focuses on interpretation, the researcher's immersion in the social settings and aims for intersubjective understanding between the researcher and the researched. Ethnography has the potential to explore the intersections of different identities that women bear and live (Skeggs 2001).

Contemporary ethnography is multi-method research involving observation, participation, archival analysis, and interviewing. In order to build a holistic picture of the lives of the disabled women based on their own interpretation of their lives, the researcher had to rely on multiple methods of data collection, which is the essence of any ethnographic account. I observed and participated in the daily activities of disabled women and their social interactions as well as used unstructured in-depth interviews with disabled women and their families. To gain a better understanding of the gender/disability ideologies operating in the context I also tried to speak to the local people about the women, their lives and what they felt about her presence in the family and in the community. These included the gram panchayat representatives, schoolteachers and other prominent people in the community like religious leaders, doctors, businessmen, etc.

The idea of using this particular research strategy came from the fact that there is very little research available on the lives of disabled women living in India, except for some studies conducted by voluntary agencies or non-governmental organizations. These were concerned mostly with the objective conditions of women with disabilities and the ways in which they were doubly discriminated in a sexist and abilist society. However, such an objective understanding of gender and disability does not allow an insight into the life-worlds of disabled women—their joys, sorrows, motivations, anxieties, social pressures and individual manifestations. As a feminist researcher, I was interested in the ways in which women with disabilities interpret and actualize gendered ideologies in their daily lives and practices and the ways in which they challenge, subvert or accept such gendered notions. The research questions led to the choice of research strategy—feminist ethnography as a means of gaining insights into lives of women whose voices have been muted and ignored, in order to reveal the ways in which disability impacts their gendered lives in different realms of life and living. As the exercise was meant to prioritize voices of disabled women, feminist ethnography seemed to be most appropriate as it allowed the research participants to have greater say over the product of the research.

This research was also stimulated by the researcher's personal experiences as well as experience of working with disabled people in the community. Feminist researchers use the strategy of 'starting from one's own experiences' and it defines our research questions, leads us to sources of useful information, gains the trust of others in doing research, and enables us to partially test our findings. Personal experience, thus, becomes the material from which the researcher develops questions and the source of finding people to study.

Thus started my journey of unravelling the voices and stories of disabled women regarding their own experiences of the complex social processes that impinge on their lives and determine the ways in which they interpret and give meaning to their daily existence.

The Social and Cultural Context

The lives of people with disabilities in India are determined, to a great extent, by their life chances as well as by their own spirit. Disability is an umbrella term for a range of physical, mental, intellectual, and sensory impairments, and the impact of each different kind of disability varies according to the severity of the disability as well as one's social and geographical location, which has implications for one's identity. There are great differences in the life experiences depending on the type and severity of disability—while women with (severe) visual impairments face discrimination in terms of employment and accessibility, they are able to handle the household work and, hence, have more scope for recognition and leading a 'woman's' life. Statistical data also reveals that it is this category of women who has more chances of getting married, as are women with mild intellectual impairments, because they can be easily included in the family set up and take up their roles as wives and mothers. For women with hearing impairments, recognition as women who are able to take up gendered social roles almost always results in desertion and abandonment, especially if the partner is not hearing impaired. For women with moderate to severe locomotor impairments, chances of leading a gendered existence is minimal, as people cannot envisage her as capable of taking on the nurturant and reproductive roles in society.

The women who are a part of this research come from varied backgrounds and inhabit different geo-spatial and social locations, ranging from the remote rural to the urban, from financially poorer families to relatively well-off families, occupying differential social statuses like being married or single, and having mild to moderate impairments to being severely disabled. The idea of degree of disability depends on the nature of impairments, involving either one or two of the limbs to all four limbs and with associated problems, but also considers the geo-spatial dimension, as the context in which a person is located determines the extent to which her daily life activities will be affected by her impairment. The women have a range of impairments which affect, to different degrees, their locomotor movements. They vary from being born with conditions like cerebral palsy[3] and arthogryposis[4] with spina bifida[5] to acquired disabilities through poliomyelitis[6] and other childhood illnesses. Although a woman's impairment may involve only one limb, her life may be grossly affected because of her geo-spatial and social location while a woman whose impairment is more severe may be less affected because of her location in a particular social context. The degree of disability corresponds to the visibility of the impairment, the extent to which the performance of different daily living activities in their everyday lives is affected in comparison to the other women around them and the ideas regarding the 'acceptable' woman. All of them were disabled either from birth or acquired their disability within the first three years of their life.

This research examines the cultural context of Bengali patriarchal society, wherein women with disabilities are constructed through common gender/disability ideologies and experience and live such constructs in the course of their daily lives. The research participants were, therefore, from both Kolkata city, which is an urban centre, and the rural South 24 Parganas, as the social context in both locations remained Bengali cultural environment. During the research, it became very clear that the disabled women had a lot to say about themselves, their perceptions, feelings, and their experiences—it was only a matter of the researcher giving importance to their voices. Feminist participant observation values openness to intimacy and striving for empathy—openness to complete transformation—which lays the ground for friendship, shared struggle and identity change. Living with the families also gave me a deeper insight into the lives and ways of living of many of the rural families which have either a family-based agro-economic activity or work in the agricultural lands as labourers or in other activities that range from fishing and *biri*[7]-making to working in the city or in factories nearby. However, the names used here are all pseudonyms in order to protect their privacy.

Outline of Chapters

This book explores the cultural representations, social processes and institutions that determine the creation and reproduction of disability in everyday socio-cultural practices, in order to gain an insight into the ways in which gender as a social construct gives particular meaning to the different areas of experience for disabled women. As both gender and disability are social constructs predicated upon physical characteristics, variations from the socially valued physical characteristics has implications for the individual's experiences in the community as the social context and cultural constructions greatly influence the experience of being male, female or having a physical impairment. The identities of people with particular bodily characteristics are constructed, sustained and maintained within societal structures and institutions, and influence their daily experiences.

The next chapter lays out the theoretical and empirical work undertaken in the realm of gender and disability studies and also reviews Indian literature on gendered ideologies that create, maintain, modify, and influence the experiences of women in their daily lives and through their socialization processes. Feminist engagement with the concept of gender and disabled theorists' exploration of the idea of disability has many parallels. Both posit a separation between the corporeal body and the social self in the dichotomies between sex and gender, and impairment and disability. Both focus on the experiences of discrimination and oppression faced by women and disabled people living in patriarchal and abilist societies. Hence, exploring the intersection of gender and disability necessarily involves exploring notions of the body, culture and society and their roles in construction and perpetuation of subjugated identities. This chapter also tries to locate feminist literature on gendered lives within the socio-cultural context of India and specifically that of West Bengal in order to ground the experiences of disabled women within such a theoretical framework.

The third chapter looks at the socialization experiences of disabled women in order to understand how the 'gender/disability' cultural context influences their lives in early childhood and adolescence. The categories of gender, disability and disabled woman are produced and represented through attributes, activities, roles, practices, and behaviour in social constructions, cultural ideologies and power relations. The gendered ideas regarding impaired bodies that construct and legitimize differences between male and female bodies and differences between female bodies based on notions of acceptability have been explored to understand the processes whereby the subjective identity of the disabled woman is constructed through socialization—how and the extent to which girls with disabilities internalize and interpret cultural ideologies about 'gender/disability', and the ways in which they construct, experience and negotiate prescribed femininities.

Chapters four and five examine the ways in which the female disabled identity is sculpted through the interaction between their impaired bodies and a gendered ability context, wherein the ideas regarding an acceptable body are internalized by disabled women themselves and sought to be refashioned either to present a semblance of femininity or question such ideologies that oppress them in their daily lives. The endeavour here is to understand the process of embodiment and explore women's emotions, feelings and experiences of sexuality, desirability, and sexual practices, marriage and motherhood. This leads to a contextualized understanding of the everyday experiences of disabled women and how these change over their life course—their social relationships and routine ways of interactions in the domains of family and household, and in the community, and their roles in the sexual division of labour.

This book illuminates the contradictory relationship between gender/ability ideologies in Bengal and India and the practices at the level of lived realities of the disabled women. Ideologies represent these women as weak, dependent, incapable of engaging in tasks like household work; perceptions about sexual division of labour influence the social construction of disabled women's bodies as lacking and deficient. Although represented as incapable and weak, the lived realities of disabled women are substantially different and their contributions to the household and family economy cannot be negated. Disabled women challenge and redefine many of these notions and ideas through the daily practices they engage in within their socio-cultural contexts. However, despite the struggles of these women in their daily lives within their homes and outside, ideologies still continue to represent them as incapable and weak, ignoring the re-assertions and re-defining of women's roles and practices within their social and cultural contexts.

Notes

1. *Kautilya's Arthashastra*, bk. II, chap. I; Fa Hien, quoted by R.C. Dutt in *A History of Civilization in Ancient India*, Delhi: Vistar Publications, 1972, p. 59.
2. An outcome of the International Year of Disabled Persons 1981 was the formulation of the World Programme of Action (WPA) concerning disabled persons, which was adopted by the UN General Assembly in December 1982. The WPA is a global strategy to enhance disability prevention, rehabilitation and equalization of opportunities, which pertains to full participation of persons with disabilities in social life and national development. It also emphasizes the need to approach disability from a human rights perspective.
3. Damage caused to brain due to prenatal, perinatal or antenatal reasons affecting the locomotor capacities and one sensory loss.
4. Congenital condition characterized by rigidity of all joints, especially the limbs.
5. Spinal deformity that prevents a person from sitting up straight.
6. Infectious disease that causes damage to nerves, leading to weakening of the muscles of the limbs and affecting mobility.
7. Local cigarettes made of unprocessed tobacco wrapped in a leaf of a particular tree.

CHAPTER II

Gender and Disability
Exploring Intersections

Gender and disability have both been theorized as complex categories that conceal power relationships between people who are perceived to be different. Presumed from the biological or physical differences between men and women, and the so-called able-bodied people and people with impairments, this difference translates itself into socio-cultural ideologies and is reflected in practice to construct, influence and discriminate between these carefully constructed artificial categories. Gender is seen to operate at all levels in order to sustain the unequal power relations within patriarchal social systems. It operates both at the macro-social level as well as the micro-political level. It may be seen being played out within the family but also outside with friends, community and at workplaces. Gender has been understood as the cultural construction of differences between the sexes. It is these culturally constructed differences that influence and organize relationships between men and women in historically specific contexts. Gender, as a system of relations, is seen as structurally embedded and ideologically enforced in all aspects of social life. Similarly, disability is mainly associated with the concept of lack or deficiency, whether mental, physical or sensory in primarily medical terms. Yet in all societies, the experience of disability is mediated by socio-cultural constructions that give meaning to impairments and influence the experiences and interactions of disabled people in different socio-historical contexts. These social constructions of disability and disabled people have a profound effect on people with disabilities, depending on the socio-cultural contexts and their definitions and interpretation of various kinds of physical and mental inadequacies as well as the resources available to facilitate the inclusion of disabled people within the community.

Conceptualizing Gender and Disability

Gender has been conceptualized as a socially constructed category that uses culturally given and accepted ideologies to distinguish between activities, behaviour, norms, and representations accorded to men and women. At the macro-structural level, gender has been conceived as a principle that seeks to constrain and direct the relations between the sexes in society. A gender divided society is seen to operate at two distinct levels—at the level of culture, involving ideologies and the cultural construction of gender differences and at the level of structure through gender roles, sex-gender systems subsuming power, and within gender relations and gender regimes. Harding (1986) argued that in every culture, gender differences are central to the way in which individuals 'identify themselves as persons, organize social relations, and symbolize meaningful natural and social processes'. Gendered social life is produced through three distinct processes: (1) gender symbolism—the result of assigning dualistic gender metaphors to various perceived dichotomies, that rarely have anything to do with sex differences; (2) gender structure—the consequence of appealing to these gender dualisms to organize social activity, dividing necessary social activities between different groups of humans; and (3) individual gender—a form of socially constructed individual identity only imperfectly correlated with the perception of sex differences (ibid.).

At the micro-political level, gender is seen as created and sustained through the interactions between gendered social beings in their daily lives, wherein gender identities are learnt, performed and negotiated by individuals in their daily lives. Gender draws attention to the ways in which sexual and social distinctions are created through day to day interaction between individuals in society and sustained by the power relations within the macro-structural arrangements of society. Gender stereotypes are developed and used by both sexes to advance their interests in various social contexts (Moore 1988). The power of gender stereotypes comes from their material reality, which helps to reinforce the social and economic conditions within which they are developed and employed. What it means to be a man or woman in a specific context takes on a normative significance (Whitehead 1981). Unequal gender relations operate within specific power regimes. They determine and are determined by socio-cultural constructions. Women's disadvantages are attributed to stereotyped customary expectations, held and internalized by both men and women. These stereotypes are promoted through families, schools, mass media and other agencies of socialization. Socialization is concerned with the transmission of behaviour, roles, attributes and beliefs to the next generation. It is done through internalization, prompted by 'socializing agents' who hold stereotypical beliefs about sex appropriate characteristics based on biology (Weinrich 1978, cited in Stanley and Wise 1982). Thus, feminine and masculine characters are produced by socialization into female and male roles—and deviants by some kind of failure in socialization.

Connell (1987) proposed a 'practice-based' theory of gender to explain the relationship between the individual and the social structure in gender formation and reproduction in order to understand gender as lived experience (Hawkesworth 1997). Gender can be understood as an interrelated set of social structures that define men and women in terms of their reproductive roles and organize social life around sex and sexuality. The main structures of the field of gender relations—division of labour, power and cathexis—are the major elements of any gender order or gender regime in society (Connell 1987). These structures, though different, interweave all the time to order social relations, shape the ideas regarding femininity and masculinity and act as a constraint on social practice.

According to Connell (1987), gender is organized through the difference between the processes of production and reproduction. The sexual division of labour necessitates the allocation of particular tasks to particular categories of people. The prior divisions of labour become established and take on the form of social rules. This persistent allocation of certain tasks and activities to women and others to men on the basis of their 'natural' aptitudes and capabilities, leads them to acquire these aptitudes and capabilities through routine performance of the same. The ideas regarding the sexual division of labour also define the nature and organization of that work. An analysis of the rules, norms and practices through which different institutions construct gender divisions and hierarchies reveals the underlying shared ideologies about the participation of men and women in public and private life. Gender hierarchies are produced dynamically through the interaction of familial gender ideologies and distinct institutional practices.

The power structure is a set of social relations, which is ideologically imposed to define a social situation. An essential part of social power entails the ability to impose a definition of the situation, to set terms by which events are understood and issues discussed, to formulate ideals and define morality or, in other words, to assert hegemony (ibid.). Within the domain of power, gender structures authority, control and coercion, by establishing hierarchies in public and private sectors. Thus, it creates a male monopoly in institutional and interpersonal violence, promoting particular modes of domestic and sexual asymmetries. The structure of cathexis, or the emotional attachment of an individual to others, forms the third structure of gender relations. Sexuality is constructed as a social category through social practices in which relationships between people are formed. Relationships in which partners can be chosen on the basis of principles of repression and prohibition (ibid.). Historically and culturally, sexual desire has been organized in terms of sexual differentiation facilitating heterosexuality. The solidarity of a heterosexual couple is formed on the basis of some kind of reciprocity, but their situations are specifically unequal. The double standard, permitting promiscuous sexuality to men and forbidding it to women, reflects the power relations existing between men and women.

The concepts of gender order and gender regime try to explain the operation of gender at the macro and intermediate levels of social organization, which is most relevant to the daily life settings like the household, the workplace, etc. A gender order refers to a historically constructed pattern of power relations between men and women, and definitions of masculinity and femininity. This order operates at the macro-societal level, and involves the creation and contestation of hegemony in definitions of sexuality (Connell 1987). A gender regime represents the play of gender relations in any given institution—the ways in which institutional practices construct various kinds of masculinity and femininity among different groups of people, the sexual division of labour within the institution, sex differences in different leisure activities, and ideologies about sexual behaviour. The pattern formed by a particular gender regime may vary from institution to institution but always within limits that reflect the balance of sexual politics in that culture. A gender regime emerges out of the continuing synthesis of relations governed by the three structures, which are inextricably linked to one another. The global relationships of power, which subordinate all women in society, must be distinguished from the micro-situations in the particular contexts, be it family, workplace or any other setting.

Feminist theorists, in the initial stages of development of feminist thought, used the concept of a 'universal woman'. This concept, which highlighted the similarities among women and their differences with men, was used as the main analytical tool to elaborate the images, attributes, activities, and appropriate behaviour associated with women in different socio-cultural contexts. However, feminists of colour and lesbians later pointed to the marginalization of their experiences within the mainstream women's movement. They drew the attention of the feminist sorority to the intersection of gender with other social identities based on human variation, like sexual orientation, class, race, and ethnicity, which shapes the perceptions, experiences and life chances of women. Every woman has multiple identities across a spectrum of cultural categories, many of which are extrapolated from physical differences (Bryson 1999; Gerschick 2000). Some feminist scholars equated femaleness with disability, as they had been denied the right to vote, own property and custody of their children. They represented female embodiment and enforced feminine comportment as delimiting women's embodied agency (Young 1990a). Femininity and race are both seen as performances of disability, endowed with the attributes of being inferior, dependent, weak, vulnerable, and incapable bodies (Garland-Thomson 2002). However, the exploration of differences among women by feminist scholars has ignored the concerns of women with disabilities, by considering disability as culturally variable and hence difficult to generalize (Ramazanoglu 1989).

The academic field of disability has also grappled with varying meanings of disability. Moving from locating the 'problem' in the individual by stressing the presence of physical or mental differences among individuals to recently acknowledging the social and cultural interpretations that echo the power relationships between the disabled and the non-disabled—all leading to marginalization and stigmatization of people with disabilities. The individual and medical models of disability attempt to explain the different ways in which disabled people have been constructed and treated, while the social model recognizes disability as socially produced by systematic patterns of exclusion that are built into the social fabric (Shakespeare 1994; Hughes and Patterson 1997). The social constructionist paradigm suggests that society creates a negative social identity for people with disabilities, which is characterized as deviant or abnormal (Asch and Fine 1988). Disability confers stigmatized status on all disabled people, as the physical characteristic becomes a master trait swamping personal differences. Thus, disability is socially imposed on physically impaired people through restrictions, ranging from individual prejudice to institutional discrimination; from inaccessible public buildings to unusable transport systems; from segregated education to excluding work arrangements.

Disability operates within culture through legal, medical, political, and literary discourses of exclusion that create the physically disabled body as an embodiment of corporeal insufficiency and a repository of social anxieties about control and identity. Disability is interlinked with complex social power relations, which implies that an individual's impairment will always be part of an embodied identity (Meekosha 1998). Attitudes, discourses and symbolic representations are critical to the reproduction of disablement, but themselves are the product of the social practices which society undertakes in order to meet its basic material needs (Oliver 1996; Gleeson 1997). The material conditions that produce the attitudes and meaning systems about disability have a great influence on the concrete experience of, and attitude towards impairment. This is because the social construction of physically impaired people as disabled people arises from the specific ways in which society organizes its basic material activities. Disability theorists have also argued that disability is a culturally fabricated narrative of the body, a system that produces subjects by differentiating and marking bodies. Impairments are multiple and are seen to impinge differently upon disabled people at different points of time, depending on a host of psychological, social and environmental factors that are all external to the biomedical condition (Silvers, Wasserman and Mahowald 1998). Disability has been described as a system for interpreting bodily variations and understanding the relationship between bodies and their environments. Other scholars represent disability as a set of practices that produce both the able-bodied and the disabled and attempt to describe the experiences of the embodied self.

The role of the body in construction, interpretation and experience of gender and disability has been increasingly stressed. The possession of a body with specific features within society becomes crucial for everyday recognition and identification of persons. It also becomes important for interpreting the interactions of individuals with and through their bodies with the world around them (Turner 1996; Davis 1997; Shakespeare 2004). The feminist movement has explored the different ways in which women, because of new articulations of the cultural construction of their bodies, were subjugated and controlled in newer ways by patriarchal ideologies. Differences between bodies assume importance for understanding embodiment as male and female bodies, inscribed with socio-cultural meanings that are derived from cultural values. They legitimize definitions of masculinity and femininity that is nurtured, sustained and sanctioned by the external social world (Dube 1989; Bagchi 1995; Thapan 1995).

The process of embodiment creates a set of constraints that are experienced differently according to gender. As a cultural statement of gender/power relations, a multiplicity of cultural meanings is attributed to the gendered body, which becomes a medium through which the oppressive cultural norms of femininity are expressed. The imposition of normative femininity upon the female body requires modes of training through disciplinary practices that operate within systems of micro-power that are fundamentally inegalitarian and asymmetrical, and are ultimately disempowering to the woman so disciplined (Bartky 1992). The bodies that women experience are always mediated by constructions, associations and images which most patriarchal socio-cultural formations accept and endorse. Patriarchal power and the gaze construct the female body within different socio-cultural contexts and power/knowledge discourses by representing female embodiment as inferior to male embodiment. Male domination and female subordination is reproduced through normative socio-cultural practices that manipulate and train the female body in docility and obedience to cultural demands, and contribute to the maintenance of power relations between the sexes (Bordo 1993, 1996).

The gender/power relations are enacted in and through women's bodies, i.e. a culture in which women must negotiate their identities vis-à-vis their appearance (Davis 1996). Therefore, women come to discipline and survey their own bodies by engaging in practices which produce their own bodies according to the dictates of idealized normative construction of feminine embodiment. The power of surveillance enforces discipline through normalization procedures that constrain women by training them to desire such controls through individual self-discipline. Women become active producers of their bodies through internalization and pursuit of continually shifting ideals of femininity propagated by cultural and media images advocating self-containment, self-monitoring and self-normalization. Women's bodies come to be tailored, by women, to conform to social ideals which are historically specific (Bartky 1992; Bordo 1995). A woman, thus, makes a statement about her body through the clothes she wears, the ways in which she chooses to enhance her facial features and the manner in which she comports herself. Feminine embodiment has been characterized by the tension between the female body as object and the female subject as embodied agent (Young 1990b). On the one hand, women are objectified bodies, as in a gendered social order, they are socially defined through their bodies. On the other hand, the body of the female subject makes her the person she is. She may or may not like certain parts or whole of her body as it may be at variance with her internalization of normative femininity (Thapan 1997). Women may not feel at ease in their bodies, as the body becomes both the site of their entrapment and the vehicle for expressing and controlling their identity. Women may regard their bodies as alien objects that are out of their control, and choose to take control over them by using technological advances to reconstruct it according to socially accepted images.

The disability movement also stressed that impairment is a social construction that excludes differences and variations in bodies and can be equally disabling in different contexts (Shakespeare and Watson 1997). The ways in which bodies interact with socially engineered environments, which includes the natural environment, the built environment, culture, the economic system, the political system, and psychological factors, and conform to social expectations determines the varying degrees of able-bodiedness or disability (Garland-Thomson 1997). People with different forms of disability experience their bodies in different ways and negotiate their identities accordingly. This is so because forms of resistance and the struggle for bodily control, independence and emancipation are differently embodied in each individual. Disability, therefore, becomes relative, its impact varying according to type and degree of impairment, socio-economic status, gender, social and geographical locations, etc.

The process of embodiment is basic to the construction of identity, whereby individuals come to be socially constructed through the meanings connected to particular bodily characteristics and the practices in which these bodies are involved. The possession of a body with specific features within society becomes crucial for everyday recognition and identification of persons. This body serves as a medium for interpreting individuals' interactions with their bodies and through their bodies with the world around them (Davis 1997). The gendered or disabled individual is seen as the result of an embodied process of thinking, feeling, perceiving, and judging, based on the body and the social meanings it has for the individual as well as for others based on the social identifications attached to it. The gendered/impaired body is located within and defined, understood and shaped by social and historical contexts. As disability is experienced in, on and through the impaired body, people with different forms of physical disability experience their bodies and negotiate their identities in different ways.

Gendered/disabled individuals come to be socially constructed through the meanings connected to particular bodily characteristics and the practices in which these bodies are involved in different social contexts. Embodiment has been defined as the process whereby the materiality of the body is interpreted through the cultural constructions that situate the body in space, time and culture. The possession of particular bodies, inscribed by markers like gender, race, sexuality, and impairment, results in the socialization into and internalization of cultural constructions and ideologies governing it, which profoundly influence construction and performance of the self through the medium of gendered bodies. Certain images of gendered/able-bodies are put forward as the norm, which are internalized and reinforced by state agencies and social institutions, like education and medicine. These normative ideas portray and legitimize certain bodily forms and shapes as more desirable in different socio-cultural contexts. Dube (1989) and Bagchi (1995) have argued that gender differences are culturally produced, inscribed and interpreted though social practices. The bodies that women experience are always mediated by constructions, associations and images, which the socio-cultural formation accepts and endorses. The female body is, therefore, produced through the cultural practices that shape and manipulate not only the physical body but also the women's lived experiences of their bodies. The acquiring of a socially acceptable body by 'normal' women becomes important to the presentation of self, in order to conform to the norms of femininity. As ideal embodied femininity is linked with social acceptability, to have a socially acceptable feminine body constructed through the appropriate practices is most crucial to a woman's sense of her identity as a female subject who is sexually desiring as well as desirable (Bartky 1992).

What has been less explored is the way in which impaired bodies influence and structure embodied experiences of people with disabilities. Disabled bodies have been excluded from theories of the body and embodiment as they are considered to lie beyond the ideals of bodily control and the capacity to strive towards 'normal' constructions of the body. The absence of disabled bodies from the conceptualization of embodiment reifies restrictive body beauty norms, and glorifies the physically flawless body. As Goffman (1963) has pointed out, individuals with bodily characteristics different from the norms of the dominant social group are considered as deviants and are devalued and subjected to processes of exclusion. People with physical disabilities constitute one such group that has been completely ignored by theories of embodiment that have assumed the presence of only non-disabled bodies. As people with impaired bodies also internalize and are subjected to the gendered disciplines of normality, they are seen as deviant both by themselves as well as by society. The social construction of disability equates people having disabled bodies with inability and asexuality, overlooking the lived reality of disabled people as gendered social beings. Recent researches in the developed countries have pointed to a deep interrelationship between impaired bodies, the ways in which they are perceived within societies, and the structuring of identities of disabled people within specific cultural contexts. Cultural constructions and power dynamics involving both female and disabled bodies greatly influence the experiences of gendered social contexts in which these women live.

Gender and Disability: Theoretical and Empirical Explorations

In the early 1980s, there was a growing awareness among feminists and disabled theorists in the Western developed countries about the neglect of women with disabilities in the relevant literature. Feminist scholars initially engaged in the process of 'bringing disabled women back in' by critiquing the male centric approach adopted by disability theorists that ignored the concerns of disabled women in society. Some feminist thinkers used the double jeopardy theory to try and unveil the different ways in which women with disabilities were more socially and economically disadvantaged than disabled men or other women. However, most of these analyses proceeded along the mainstream social structural-functional model defined by disabled men (Lloyd 1992). Thus, disabled women were seen as victims of a sexist and ableist society, which places them in a position of double disadvantage as impairment negates their womanhood (Vernon 1999). It was argued that disabled women experience simultaneous handicaps, of being female in a patriarchal society and disabled in an ableist society (Hanna and Rogovsky 1991, cited in Lloyd 1992). Two stigmatized statuses converge in the lives of disabled women, further diminishing an already diminished gender status. The double jeopardy perspective was very effective in highlighting different problems faced by disabled women in their pursuit of a more meaningful existence. The identification of the specific problems of disabled women and the 'disabling' structures and socio-cultural attitudes also provided new directions for research, policy and interventions.

Disabled women are doubly disadvantaged economically, socially and psychologically in relation to the 'single' minority reference groups they are a part of disabled men and non-disabled women. For disabled women, there emerges a dilemma of identity, which may be resolved by creating a hierarchy of inequalities with disability assuming the greatest significance (Deegan and Brooks 1985; Asch and Fine 1985, 1988; Lonsdale 1990; Lloyd 1992). The presence of a disability was seen as more severely handicapping for women than men. This differential experience was attributed to the limited role choices and role models available to disabled women. Thus, disabled women experience 'rolelessness', or the absence of sanctioned social roles and the institutional means to achieve them, and this characterizes the circumstances of women with disabilities in society.

Most of the studies aimed at exploring the extent to which disabled women were able to fulfil the traditional gender role expectations within society. The research on women with disabilities has concentrated mainly on locomotor and sensory disabilities as these groups of women were seen as capable of, yet denied the avenues for attaining traditional gender roles. The broad areas of investigation were the traditional spheres of reproduction and nurturing, and education and employment. The thrust of these studies was to determine whether women's roles as nurturers, wives and homemakers were seen as appropriate for women with disabilities, and the limitations faced by disabled women within the traditional women's sphere, that demonstrated the restricted social options available to them (Traustadottir 1990).

Women with disabilities have historically been denied the traditional roles of homemakers and mothers (Asch 2001). As disability is linked with asexuality, marital and reproductive prospects of disabled women are seriously affected. Many studies found that compared to disabled men and non-disabled women, disabled women are more likely never to marry or marry late (Asch and Fine 1988). Only five of the forty-five women interviewed by Matthews (1983) were married and there is hardly a mention of marriage in a collection of first-person accounts written by more than sixty women (Traustadottir 1990). Asch and Fine (1988) report only one group of women with disabilities that is more likely to be married than men of the same disability group. This group is women with mental retardation. Women with disabilities are also more likely to be divorced or abandoned because they are seen as incapable of caring for the family and children. Men are more likely to divorce their disabled wives, while the converse occurs rarely because traditionally women have been ascribed the role of carers (Safilios-Rothschild 1976; Asch and Fine 1988; Hannaford 1989). When disability occurs after marriage, men are much more likely to divorce their wives who become disabled, while the marriage rarely breaks down if the man becomes disabled (Hannaford 1989). When disabled women do become mothers, they encounter more difficulties because of the non-disabled world's assumption that their disability is an impediment to their mothering role. Thus, many disabled women do not perceive marriage or traditional female roles as desirable, mainly because access of disabled women to traditional roles is very restricted, whereas non-disabled women are more likely to have the possibility of choosing between traditional and non-traditional lifestyles (Asch and Fine 1988).

In the areas of education and employment, most studies found disabled women to be grossly disadvantaged. Disabled women from differing social situations felt that rehabilitation programmes were designed to suit disabled men's aspirations for recovering their masculinity and sexuality, while the needs of disabled women were often ignored (Begum 1992; Morris 1993a). Disabled men are more likely to be referred to vocational training schools than disabled women. Most studies reveal that disabled women have less access to the benefits to be gained from governments and other organizations than disabled men. Women with disabilities receive less education than non-disabled women and men with disabilities (Bowe 1984, cited in Traustadottir 1990). Although people with disabilities face discrimination in employment, women with disabilities fare worse than disabled men in terms of training as well as employment. The belief that men are breadwinners and women homemakers has a great influence on training and employment patterns of disabled men and women. Disabled women are more likely to be unemployed, or engage in unskilled labour that also pays less (Lonsdale 1990). The disadvantage, discrimination and inappropriateness of employment structures that disabled people encounter are faced by women as an inevitable consequence of their gender. For disabled women, the disadvantages of being female and disabled compound each other (Hanna and Rogovsky 1991, cited in Lloyd 1992). Women's powerlessness is, thus, confirmed by their gender and their disability within a hostile economy and a discriminatory society (Asch and Fine 1988).

In Asian and African countries, most of the research on people with disabilities have been conducted by non-governmental organizations (NGOs). Since the focus is on the rehabilitation services provided, these NGOs do not make any distinction between men and women with disabilities. However, the NGO reports reveal that physical, social, psychological and other disadvantages caused by disability have a strong gender dimension and are dealt with through gendered approaches in the particular cultural and structural contexts of the Third World countries. The disability of an individual interacts with the different gender role expectations determined by historical, religious, ideological, ethnic, economic and cultural factors (Bacquer and Sharma 1997). However, most of these studies have ignored the effect of class, caste, regional affiliations and type and degree of disability, while exploring the concerns of disabled people. In order to gain a deeper understanding of the daily lived experiences of disabled men and women, through an insight into cultural ideologies and social constructions of gender and disability in India, one must also take into account the influence of caste, class, religion, ethnic and other ideologies in structuring perceptions of gender and disability. Most studies have adopted the 'double discrimination' approach that identifies problems faced by women with disabilities in their strife to achieve traditional social roles. The disparities are evident in rehabilitation of women with disabilities in the fields of education and employment, and independence or self-reliance achieved by them. The predominant concerns revealed are regional variations in the social attitudes, differences in upbringing, the scope for realization of gender roles within the family and abuse of women with disabilities.

Indian and other Asian studies have corroborated the findings of studies conducted in the Western countries. It has been found that disabled women have lesser access to rehabilitation services like health care, education, vocational training opportunities, mainly because of their social and cultural isolation and the reluctance to approach the predominantly male service providers (NCPEDP-NAB 1999; Thomas and Thomas 2002). There are rural urban differences in the ways in which women with disabilities face double discrimination. In rural areas, disabled girls are more prone to life and health risks because of parental apathy towards the girl child (Maqbool 2003). In India, a sizeable number of girls and women with disabilities have been reported to be permanently in poor health, with the added risk of falling ill frequently (Bacquer and Sharma 1997). It has been found that very few disabled women approach doctors for medical advice in India and that too only in case of emergencies (Sengupta and Ghosh 2003). Although in rural areas, disabled women are more stigmatized than disabled men, the gender bias operates more strongly in the impersonal urban environment. The informal community ties in rural areas act as a safety net for disabled girls, who may be more vulnerable to the apathetic attitudes in the urban centres.

In the strong patriarchal communities of Asia, the father or the male head of the family takes decisions on important matters like medical treatment, education, training, and independence, even though it is the mother who cares for the disabled daughter. In cultures where daughters are looked down on, a disabled daughter is seen as a curse as she has to contend with disappointment over her birth as well as her disability (Ghai 2002). Often disabled girls are forbidden to leave the home as her presence brings shame and dishonour to the family. However, restrictions on disabled women vary culturally as well as by the type of disability. In spite of the external cultural restrictions, girls with disabilities have been found to participate equally in most types of household work carried on within the home (Abu-Habib 1997).

Other studies, however, have revealed that disabled women, because of their assumed asexuality, enjoy greater freedom in comparison to able-bodied women. They are encouraged to take up non-traditional pursuits as they are deemed unfit for traditional female roles. Yet these women continue to remain outside the pale of public esteem and regard, even when engaged in successful careers. In contrast disabled men are usually supported by their families and are involved in paid jobs (Abu-Habib 1997; Ghosh 2002). However, in the Middle East, class and gender affect the visibility chances of disabled people. Here disabled men and disabled women from affluent families participate equally in the community affairs and social life. While disabled men become key figures in the community, very few disabled women gain social recognition. In Palestine, men who become disabled as result of war are hailed as heroes by their local communities, but women disabled during war are not treated in the same manner (Abu-Habib 1997).

The double disadvantage theory, however, took for granted the cultural constructions of women and focused on the extent to which disabled women were able to live up to such ideals. It ignored the fact that gender and disability operate as structures of oppression for both disabled men and women, primarily because dependence/independence are projected as the socio-cultural meanings of what it is to be a 'man' or a 'woman'. The concept of double jeopardy, thus, shifts attention away from the role of non-disabled people and social institutions in creating and maintaining devalued ideas about disabled women by accepting the culturally given and accepted definitions of gender and disability (Morris 1993b; Sheldon 1999). This double discrimination perspective failed to question the acceptability of gender roles as a framework for understanding the experiences of disabled women. The internal differentiation among women themselves was also ignored, based on an assumption that class, race and ethnic backgrounds did not have any impact on the lives of disabled women. Some disabled scholars have challenged the double jeopardy theory, as it projects women with disabilities as passive victims. They argue that as both gender and disability are social constructs based on physical characteristics, gender plays an important role in determining how a person's disability is perceived (Abu-Habib 1997; Begum 1992). As gender and disability identities interact, men and women with physical impairments in particular social contexts experience power relationships that greatly impact their lived reality. Gender and disability ideologies permeate all aspects of life, and determine power relations in the form of social hierarchies, attitudes, and distribution of resources within households and at the community level. Gendered experiences of disability may be seen as reinforcing inequalities between men and women as both gender and disability are aspects of social identity, which leads to potential marginalization within a society that is designed to be run by able-bodied men (Abu-Habib 1997; Ferri and Gregg 1998).

'Feminist Disability Studies'

The newly emergent field of feminist disability studies has attempted to redress the dearth of research on the intersection of gender and disability by conceptualizing disability as a blend of socially constructed identities and a form of embodiment that interacts with the material and social environments (Garland-Thomson 2005). Feminist Disability Studies demonstrates that disability, like race and gender, is a system of representation that marks bodies with a wide range of varying physical characteristics and subjective experiences as subordinate, and which produces and sustains ascribed, achieved and acquired identities. Thus, feminist disability theorists consider that disability, like gender, pervades all aspects of culture—the social institutions, cultural identities, socio-cultural and religious practices and political positions that influence the shared experience of embodiment. The main thrust of feminist disability studies is to try to understand how these multiple systems, that operate to support an imaginary norm and resultant power relations, intertwine, redefine and mutually constitute one another. Disabled feminist scholars have used feminism as a theoretical perspective for examining gender as an ideological and material category that interacts with other social identities, taking into consideration the particularities of embodiment, history and location (ibid.). Disabled feminists have also explored the theoretical concerns of representation, embodiment, identity and intersectionality from the perspective of the disabled woman subject

(Wendell 1996).Thus, the aim of feminist disability studies is to augment and correct traditional feminist literature which sometimes misrepresents, ignores or conflicts with the concerns of women with disabilities (Garland-Thomson 2002, 2005).

CULTURAL CONSTRUCTIONS AND EXPERIENCES OF MEN AND WOMEN WITH DISABILITIES

Gender and disability are both equally oppressive for disabled men and women. But this affects them in different ways as the able-bodied ideologies represent and construct a gendered notion of disability based on the constructions of masculinity and femininity within particular socio-cultural contexts. The public imagination that constructs the good citizen as male, white, active, fit and able, conceives of people with disabilities, in complete contrast, as inactive, disabled, passive citizens (Meekosha and Dowse 1997; Lonsdale 1990). Disabled people, stereotyped as helpless dependents, are seen as incapable of leading socially and economically productive lives. The gendering process passes on to the disabled individual, cultural values regarding masculinity and femininity, endowed with particular character traits that are seen as 'natural' for the gendered person. Such stereotyped cultural ideas regarding disability greatly influence the lives of both disabled men and women, as disability is equated with inability to live 'complete' or 'normal' lives. The relationship between masculinity and femininity as social constructs is indicative of the way in which the so-called able-bodied society defines physical impairment. The dominant images mirror the gendered role expectations for men and women—men as active, aggressive and instrumental and women as passive, invisible and expressive (Lonsdale 1990).

The lack of perceived masculine and feminine character traits structures the experiences of disability for men and women in all cultures. Cultural representation confers a devalued status on disabled men as they are considered to be incapable of conforming to cultural definitions of masculinity which comprises of positive qualities like strength, autonomy and authority. Images of disability detract from the image of man as an assertive and confident person. This was one of the main reasons for hiding the disability of President Roosevelt of the US from the public and he was never shown using a wheelchair, which is the ultimate symbol of dependency and lack of autonomy (Campling 1983; Asch and Fine 1988). However, gendered cultural representation ensures a more positive identity for men with disabilities as they are assumed to embody some 'masculine' character traits.

The experience of disability for disabled men is, thus, different from the way in which women experience disability, because men and women, despite their disabilities, are socialized differently. Both disabled men and women experience negative, yet different effects of gender stereotyping as they fail to conform to traditionally and socially agreed norms of beauty and strength (Lloyd 1992). Disabled men experience masculinity as an oppressive social construct as they fail to measure up to socially accepted definitions (Asch and Fine 1988). As they have limited access to cultural resources to negotiate the gender order, disabled men do not enjoy all the power and privileges that are accorded to non-disabled men (Shakespeare 1999). Two sets of social dynamics converge in the lives of men with physical disabilities—the demands embodied in hegemonic masculinity (Connell 1987, 1995) and the stigmatization of people with disabilities (Gerschick and Miller 1995, 1997). Men with disabilities face a conflict of choice between the two markers of identity, masculinity and disability, and can use masculinity to resist the disabled identity and, thus, fulfil socially powerful male roles (Asch and Fine 1988). Studies on masculinity and disability reveal that disabled men can subvert the devalued disabled status by reformulating and redefining hegemonic masculine characteristics on their own terms, for example by describing independence, not as self-reliance and autonomy but as being able to take charge and control of one's life. Some disabled men also counter the devaluation by adopting particular predominant masculine attributes or rejecting commonly held cultural standards, thereby either creating their own principles and practices or denying the importance of masculinity in their lives (Gerschick and Miller 1995, 1997). Many disabled men may, therefore, reject dominant masculine traits like strength, while identifying masculinity with mental prowess and intelligence.

On the other hand, women with disabilities in both their identifications are represented as weak, passive and dependent, and this partial congruity between the character traits associated with both femininity and disability has significant consequences for them in terms of the unequal power relationship that characterizes their social experience. Disabled women, usually defined in terms of biological anomaly and limitation, fall far short of the traditional female stereotype because they may not conform to the societal specifications regarding physical appearance, which is more significant for women than for men in a sexist society. A woman is expected to be beautiful as well as capable of fulfilling the sexual/social demands of her husband/family. Very few women with disabilities are seen as conforming to the stereotypes of feminine physical appearance. A disabled woman is labelled a failure, as she does not fulfil the accepted norms of beauty and gendered notions about women (Asch and Fine 1988).

Women, disabled at birth or from early childhood, find themselves defined predominantly by their physical condition and are less expected to conform to gendered expectations of femininity as they are excluded from the sex-gender system, where a woman is judged by her physical appearance and her functional utility in any relationship. The figure of the disabled woman becomes the third cultural term defined by the original pair of the masculine figure and the feminine figure which are represented as opposites. The disabled female figure is seen as the antithesis of both the masculine figure and the 'normal' woman and is posited as both inside and outside the category of women (Garland-Thomson 1997).

The sex-gender system has always represented women as nurturers in their roles as daughters, wives and mothers. In almost all parts of the world, women have the primary responsibility as carers for children, spouses, parents or relations who have illnesses or disabilities. While feminist scholars have critiqued the family as an oppressive institution through which socially constructed feminine roles are established and maintained, most women still strive to conform to the appropriate gender roles they are ascribed. Disability profoundly affects a woman's chances of a 'normal' life in the private sphere because social restrictions and bodily impairments undermine their capacity to fulfil the caring roles. Although disabled women strive to attain traditional gender roles as it represents a means of becoming equal with all other women, they are considered to be unfit to be a homemaker, wife and mother because of their assumed functional limitations (Begum 1992; Morris 1993b). Disabled women are, thus, not freed, but denied access to the patriarchal sex-gender system as they are considered to be incapable of fulfilling the nurturant roles, which affect their prospects for leading a 'normal' social life.

Within traditional patriarchal communities, disabled women often find themselves left out of gendered representations and the symbolic order. As women with disabilities are denied recognition as sexual beings, they are also exempted from sexist notions of womanhood. Thus, disabled women could feel less pressure from sex role stereotypes and resist some of the oppressive dual dependency images imposed by society (Lonsdale 1990). Yet if a disabled woman is non-feminine, it is attributed to her disability and not to her choice to be a feminist. On the other hand, feminism's revaluing of customary social roles of women debars disabled women from a womanhood narrowly defined by roles from which they are excluded by virtue of the social construction of their impairments (Silvers 2000). Thus, women with disabilities face double invisibility both as subjects and objects of desire, as the social perception of disabled people as asexual impinges on their identity and experience as feminine beings (Ferri and Gregg 1998). Women with disabilities may, as a result, portray themselves as ultra-feminine to counter such stereotyping and find themselves subscribing to traditional notions of femininity more than non-disabled women, mainly because avenues for subversion of their disabled and gendered identity may not be available to them (Begum 1992).

The cultural value of men and women depends on the different social and functional roles that they are assigned by religio-cultural ideologies. In cultures where marriage and family bestows primary social status to the individual in the community, marriage prospects of disabled people are affected by their disability as well as their gender. Disabled men are more likely to get married and lead 'normal' family lives whereas disabled women's marriage chances are profoundly affected by their disability (Bhambani 2003; Thomas and Thomas 2002; Abu-Habib 1997). Disabled men, as receivers of able-bodied brides, are valued more than disabled women, and feel that they are perfectly eligible for marriage and parenthood as they could provide for their wives. In traditional societies, where marriages are arranged based on criteria of physical beauty and capacity to serve the marital family, disabled women are disqualified on grounds of both physical imperfection as well as functional limitations. Disabled women grapple with the cultural stereotyping that forces them to accept that marriage and motherhood confers a purpose and identity, which they are denied because of their disability. They are seen as dependent and in need of care rather than caring for others, and are also considered to be unsuitable for bearing and rearing healthy children (Bacquer and Sharma 1997; Ghosh 2002; Bhambani 2003). As a result, parents usually look for disabled or widowed men for an alliance with their disabled daughter, and also compensate the groom's family adequately for gifting an 'incomplete' woman to the family (Abu-Habib 1997; Bacquer and Sharma 1997; Ghai 2002; Thomas and Thomas 2002).

THE GENDERED/DISABLED BODY

The bodies of people with disabilities make them vulnerable to being denied recognition as women and men. For boys and men, body image is linked to whether their bodies will do certain things, whereas for girls and women the predominant concern largely is whether their bodies will look right and be acceptable. Both men and women are affected by messages exhorting them to take responsibility for maintaining their bodies. Moreover, disability also connotes the lack of control over bodily movements which is projected as undesirable for any person (Stone 1995). For a disabled man, weakening and atrophy of the body threatens the cultural values of masculinity: strength, activeness, speed, virility, stamina and fortitude. Men with disabilities are marginalized and stigmatized because they undermine the typical role of the body. Men's bodies allow them to demonstrate the socially valuable characteristics of toughness, competitiveness and ability. The bodies of men with disabilities reveal that they are at odds with the expectations of the dominant culture. Men's bodies have always been at issue for concepts such as strength, potency, and physical activity. True masculinity is almost always thought to proceed from men's bodies—to be inherent in a male body or to express something about a male body (Connell 1995).

As women have been traditionally identified with their bodies, they are taught from early childhood to be conscious of body shape, size, hair and facial features, which are determined by culturally prescribed appearance norms. Such norms portray defective bodies as inadequate, and reinforce the traditional conceptualization of the disabled body as deficient and in need of reconstruction or 'improvement' (Begum 1992; Garland-Thomson 1994, 2002). The disciplinary practices of physical normalcy, which are learnt early and unconsciously, create a standard of physical normality, as the disciplines of femininity create the ideal women (Wendell 1996). Hillyer (1993) feels that all women, including women with disabilities, are evaluated by a body code that requires strict adherence to culturally constructed feminine disciplinary practices. From an early age, women, and disabled women especially, learn to feel uncomfortable with their bodies (Campling 1983; Rimassa 1997). Feminine body ideals and standardization of female bodies tend towards the normate—the corporeal incarnation of culture's collective, unmarked, normative characteristics (Garland-Thomson 2002). Disabled women are just as likely to internalize and be influenced by dominant norms and values about attractiveness and physical appearance as other women, and perceive themselves to be lacking the popular standard of beauty.

For many women with disabilities, an 'ideal' body may be difficult to attain because it implies certain basic features such as being of an appropriate height or having two ordinarily functioning arms and legs. The twin ideologies of normalcy and beauty posit female and disabled bodies, as pliable ones to be shaped infinitely to conform to a set of standards called normal and beautiful. While all women are subjected to disciplines of femininity, women with physical disabilities have to contend with the subtle message that their bodies won't ever measure up aesthetically or functionally in the physical environment (Tighe 2001). Disabled women may find that their bodies, denied recognition as sexual objects, are nonetheless objectified for manipulation and control (Begum 1992). The authority assumed by the state and the patriarchal medical and social system are all aimed at normalizing the disabled female body (Meekosha 1998; Silvers 2000). For disabled women, the normalizing medical system often represents a denial of their individuality and their self, because of the stress on 'curing' and removing impairment through unnecessary surgical procedures (Lonsdale 1990). However, the internalization of dominant ideas of female subordination by disabled women themselves as well as their subjection to medical interventions together colludes towards the normalization of the imperfect female body (Meekosha 1998).

While the bodies of women and disabled men are reduced to biological lack of functioning or deficiency, for a woman with disability, the comparison with other women's bodies becomes even more oppressive. While non-disabled women's bodies may be unequal, they can still be healthy and beautiful and, thus, signify reproduction of domination of able-bodied gender ideologies. But the bodies of disabled women signify the opposite—the inability to reproduce and hence, ugly. Thus, disabled women become more vulnerable to the myth of bodily perfection as their bodies are denied recognition or provoke disgust and are relegated to spaces outside mainstream society (Meekosha 1998). Most women with disabilities have ambivalent feelings towards their bodies, privileging mind over body in order to subvert the disciplines of normality (Tighe 2001). For physically disabled women, distancing themselves from their bodies is a necessity as well as a luxury as performing major life functions also draws attention to the impaired body. However, disabled women are also forced to concede that body and mind are inextricably linked and may view the perfect female body as an oppressive construct propounded by an ableist society (Lonsdale 1990; Begum 1992; Ferri and Gregg 1998; Stone 1995).

Disabled women are, therefore, unable to deny their physicality, as they are identified through their bodies especially in traditional cultures where physical perfection and functionality carry high value. Women with disabilities find it very difficult to escape the entrapment of physical/mental and socio-cultural inadequacies (Limaye 2003). They have to contend not only with the way men look at women but also with the way society stares at disabled people, stripping them of any semblance of resistance (Ghai 2002). The prevalent ideals of female bodies make it difficult for women with disabilities to resist the dominant order. Society forces disabled women to define roles for themselves based on the images and values of their social context, thereby forging new subjugated identities within the restraints imposed by society. The Indian cultural traditions equate disability with de-sexing; this is evident from the Punjabi cultural practice that forbids ordinary girls to share a room with their male cousins but allows disabled girls to do so (Ghai 2002). The control over sexuality of women with disabilities extends even beyond the family, when residential institutions sometimes force them to undergo hysterectomies.

A major area of concern that has emerged in developing countries is the abuse of women with disabilities within the home, at the institutions they may be living or working in, by medical professionals and within the community. Disabled women are liable to be subjected to physical, sexual and emotional abuse regardless of age, class and type of disability. They are more vulnerable to domestic violence, whether from the parents, siblings or husband and his family, and their social isolation usually acts as a barrier to seeking help. As disabled women are in a state of physical, social and economic dependence, they experience abuse for longer periods, and are likely to be abused by a greater number of perpetrators, with women with disabilities living in the cities at increased risk. The violations against disabled girls go unreported as they as well as their families do not have the courage to approach the legal and police systems (Bacquer and Sharma 1997; Maqbool 2003).

Gendered Relations in India: Focus on Bengal

The women's movement in India laid great stress on the country's specific cultural traditions and social structure as the form of male supremacy was very different, with different implications for gender relations. The specific form of male supremacy in India affected men's views and treatment of women as well as how women saw themselves and constructed their demands. The primary influences on the formation of gender relations were the patriarchal family organization, the formation of caste hierarchy and the impact of foreign domination (Liddle and Joshi 1986). In India, male supremacy was not a natural or inevitable development in the history of gender relations, but was a result of a struggle between the female power principle and the idea of the male as the dominant source of power. The idea of women as powerful was accommodated into the patriarchal culture and retained its visibility, both in the brahminical[1] and Islamic traditions (ibid.). Patriarchy refers to the particular system of family organization, which includes patrilineal inheritance, the married sons and their families staying in the father's house and the authority of the father over the women and younger men supported by a cultural tradition, which emphasizes the supremacy of the male power principle. South Asian societies are characterized by strong patriliny, patrilocality, male authority and control over resources (Mukhopadhyay and Seymour 1994). Most South Asian women, rooted in patrilineal, patri-virilocal kinship with limited rights over resources and virtually no inheritance rights, dependent, secluded and segregated, their sexuality managed by men, do not have any choices or have only limited choices.

The status of women in Bengal has traditionally been low, as is evident from documented sources from early and medieval period, where women have been represented only as consorts and the royal sisters of kings of different dynasties like the Pala and Sena dynasties. In the traditional social hierarchy of the Hindus, women and the shudras (lowest in the caste order, untouchables) were the two lowest categories as both were denied access to the Vedic religious rites. The basic rules for women's behaviour mentioned in the Laws of Manu written in the early Christian era stress the need to control female sexuality. Women, because of their evil inclinations and birth, are to be kept under control of men at all stages of their lives by fathers, husbands and sons. The ideal women are those who protect their chastity and virtue as daughters, wives and widows (Wadley 1999). Manu described women as having no sense of morality and no scruples regarding sexual matters and as always ready to sleep with any man (Murshid 1983). Hence, fathers had to give away their daughters in marriage before she reached puberty, as controlling the woman's sexuality remained the responsibility of males of her family (Mazumdar 1994). In the texts of the twelfth century, there are references to the *kulin pratha*, or pre-puberty marriage of brides with grooms thrice their age. The texts have references to women as having very low social status other than that derived from their position in the family, and no legal rights as they were not allowed to inherit. The only exception were widows who were allowed to 'use' their husband's property if there was no male heir (Forbes 2005).

During Islamic and later British rule in Bengal, there was a movement towards Sanskritization. This involved refinement of social behaviour, adoption of purer ritual symbols like the wearing of the sacred thread, prohibitions on widow remarriage, introduction of dowry, and child marriage. The effect of such Sanskritization was greater restrictions on women as they came to represent the honour of the community that needed to be protected. The un-freedom of women became more widely prevalent across all social strata in late colonial Bengal (Bandyopadhyay 2004). Class classifications establishing a rigid hierarchy were re-introduced. Some of the different aspects of social restructuring that are seen during this period were hypergamy, child marriage, polygamy of men with attractive caste attributes and an increase of sati (Mazumdar 1994). While the public space became the sphere of economic and political activity for men, women were confined to the household (Urquhart 1927).

In India, over the last three centuries, there has been a complex process of construction of gender through cultural symbols, social ideologies and invoking of the so-called indigenous belief systems. According to Bagchi (1995), Indian womanhood is based on a multilayered accretion of myths that serves patriarchy in both its global and local manifestations. There was a tendency to 'essentialize' and homogenize the Indian woman, such that women's role in reproduction was seen as natural and became a means to justify their continued domination by men. Early in the nineteenth century, the 'woman question' became central to discussions about Indian civilization and influential British writers referred to the treatment of women in condemning Indian religions, culture, and society as inferior. The British had referred to cultural practices like sati, child marriage, widowhood, polygamy, and prohibitions on education as degenerate and 'barbaric'. Hence in the early and mid-nineteenth-century Bengal, social reformers like Ishwar Chandra Vidyasagar and Rammohun Roy along with movements like the Brahmo Samaj sought to modernize the Indian woman. Most of them belonged to the upper caste educated *bhadralok*[2] groups who had been well exposed to Western ideas (Chatterjee 1993).

The social reformers who tried to ameliorate the condition of Indian women through legislation pleaded the purity of Indian women in order to save them from the brutal clutches of Hindu orthodoxy (Sarkar 1994). The cultural representation of Indian women as pure and chaste and in need of protection from the colonial masters also led to the re-visualization of women as the symbol of female power or Shakti prevalent in Hindu ideology, to establish the regime of caste, class and gender oppression. But such gender ideologies further served to 'essentialize' and thereby homogenize women through systems of knowledge, beliefs, institutions, and socio-economic formations. The familial class/caste agenda within which the gendered cultural constructions were presented helped to establish the upper class, upper caste Hindu male as the social norm against which women of the same class, and men and women of the lower castes were to be measured (Bannerji 2002; Karlekar 1991).

The social reform movements against sati (burning of widows on the pyre of their dead husbands) and introducing widow remarriage were partially successful, but received only tepid support from the upper caste Hindu gentry, in Bengal. Most of the upper and mid-ranking castes in Bengal practised child marriage and forbade widow remarriage in the nineteenth century. At the end of the nineteenth century it was only the lowest menial groups like the *doms* and *bagdis* who practised widow remarriage without any stigma attached to it while the rest of the Bengali Hindu society strictly forbade this custom. Brahminical upper caste status was asserted by distinguishing marriage customs and control of female sexuality from those of the lower castes. The culture of the *pativrata* or the one who remains faithful to her husband was propagated as the norm. Lower caste widows were permitted to remarry but not those of the upper castes. Divorce initiated by the wife was possible in the lower castes but forbidden among the brahminical upper castes till the 1950s. Polyandry, levirate and widow re-mating were common among many tribes and peasant groups, therefore ipso facto unacceptable as upper caste brahminical practice. Women's education was initially condemned by all strata of society, as they feared that it would destroy family discipline and culture (Chakraborty 1998). Even when the idea gained popularity, the aim of education for women was to find educated and well-placed grooms, and to produce better wives, mothers and companions for their husbands.

The nationalist movement redefined Indian womanhood in order to argue for the superiority of Indian culture over that of the West and to establish its claim for sovereignty (Bagchi 1990; Tharu and Lalitha 1991; Chatterjee 1993). In order to project the superiority of the Indian identity over the colonial masters, nationalist leaders separated the domain of culture into two spheres, the material and the spiritual, which corresponded to an ideologically more powerful dichotomy between the inner and outer. The inner/outer distinction separated social space into the *ghar* and *bahir*, the home and the world. The *bahir* was seen as the domain of the male, of practical considerations and dominated by the profane activities of the material world, while the home was posited as the representation of one's true identity, one's spiritual self, and women became the representation of this inner/spiritual domain. This ideological distinction between the public/private, the *bahir/ghar* and the material/spiritual led to the identification of social roles by gender and spheres of operation of men and women in Bengali society (Chatterjee 1993). The strict segregation of private feminine spaces from the public male areas led to the formulation of two completely different worlds of physical experience and quality of life, governed by varying norms and expectations which affected the relationships between the sexes and created distinct spheres of functions and influence. From this period of early nationalism and high imperialism emerged the figure of the chaste uppercaste, upper- and middle-class Hindu woman, who in her role initially as wife, and later as mother, became the supreme emblem of a consolidated Hindu nationalist selfhood (Mazumdar 1994; Mookerjea-Leonard 2005).

The works of Bengali authors of this period reflected the traditional gender ideology, which identified respectable women with privacy and domesticity, and constantly propagated the socially conservative ideal of the Bengali Hindu girl who had completed basic middle or high school, deeply religious, married at an early age, modest in behaviour, showing deep respect and devotion to her husband and ready to sacrifice her life if the domestic situation demanded it (Bagchi 1990; Chatterjee 1993). Young women, in training for becoming a *bhadramahila*,[3] were encouraged to be educated in order to gain particular skills and relevant values. These values or womanly virtues included chastity, self-sacrifice, submission, devotion, kindness, patience and the labours of love while the new skills were of orderliness, thrift, cleanliness, hygiene and the ability to run the household according to the new physical and economic conditions.

Orthodox Bengali society has been largely patrilineal with the household being patrilocal and women having little status or place as an individual. It was only under the protection of her father or husband that she had a clearly defined position and prestige (Urquhart 1927; Engels 1996). For women in Bengal, all relationships centred around the men in the family, be it the father, brother or later the husband and son. The emphasis on a woman's behaviour is in relationship to men, wife/husband, mother/son, daughter/father and sister/brother (Wadley 1999). In Bengal's cultural tradition, women have always been viewed as goddesses like Durga and Kali, with considerable power and independence (Karlekar 1991). However, the Bengal Renaissance and the nationalist movement witnessed the recasting of women as mothers with the social responsibility of spirituality, which curtailed the tendency for independent action. Women were portrayed as docile, self-denying and showing complete deference to the control of men in their lives. From then on, the nature of gender relations and women's roles have been clearly defined in Bengali society.

Women's lives can be divided into three phases: daughter, wife and mother. Non-feminist analyses represent women's lives as assuming significance only after marriage, ensuring which was the sacred obligation of the father (Urquhart 1927; Roy 1972; Fruzzetti 1990). Feminist accounts of the nineteenth century document the ways in which the birth of daughter cast a pall of gloom as daughters are considered to be inauspicious. In most families, whether middle or lower caste, daughters were married off at a very young age in order to improve ritual status, to relieve themselves of the burden of feeding their daughters and to cater for marriage expenses as soon as possible (Engels 1996). Although till the early twentieth century, in many Bengali families the birth of daughter was greeted with sorrow (Chakraborty 1963; Ghosh 1986); later researches (Roy 1972; Bagchi, Guha and Sengupta 1997) have found that most families do not consider a daughter's birth as a sad affair. According to Bagchi et al. (1997), 'it is not that girls are unwanted today as they were earlier, although there are few who want only daughters'. Though there is a preference for sons, once the girl arrives, the child is loved for her own sake and there is no preferential treatment (Cormack 1961). Bengali culture is well known for its *vatsalya sneha* or the affection for one's offspring and the mother-child relationship takes on precedence over all other familial mores (Bagchi 1990; Roy 1972). However, the position of the girl child in the family is specifically unequal from that of her brother, as daughters of a line are expected to treat residence in their paternal house as temporary as her membership in her father's agnatic group is neither permanent nor complete. A woman is, therefore, considered to be a peripheral member of her descent group (Dube 2001).

The life of a woman can be divided into two parts: one before her marriage spent at her *baper bari* (natal home) and the other after, at her *sasur bari* (affinal home). The first period is brief compared to her second but the early years leave a strong mark on a girl's life (Urquhart 1927). Fathers are known to be very gentle and kind to the young girls and often refer to their daughters as the little mother or *lakshmi* (Goddess of wealth and prosperity) (Roy 1972; Östör and Fruzzetti 1982; Ghosh 1986). As a woman is primarily defined in marital terms, she is relatively free only as her father's daughter (Bannerji 2002). The young *kumari* (unmarried girl in her pre-puberty years) is allowed to roam about freely in her father's house and her relationship with her brothers and other men of the family is affable, open and easy (Östör and Fruzzetti 1982). Dyson and Moore (1983) found that in Bengal strong kinship ties meant that women's movements were less rigidly controlled and women, thus, interacted more regularly with their natal kin. There are two models for women to follow, one for young unmarried girls and the other for married women who are expected to model their lives on those of their mother or mother-in-law. There are neither aspirations nor models associated with spinsterhood in this society.

In Bengal, with its stress on motherhood as the only goal for women, the domestic arena is recognized as the most suitable for girls. Bengali girls are trained by female relatives and kinswomen from a very early age to fulfil her future role as a good wife and mother by the family and society at large (Roy 1972; Bagchi 1993; Chakraborty 1998). Within the family, girls learn to help with the household work and domestic chores as well as learning of her duties and obligations, and are trained to modify expectations and adjust behaviour accordingly (Cormack 1961; Bagchi, Guha and Sengupta 1997). Sex role typing still expects daughters to grow up in the image of their mothers, learning womanly skills and feminine virtues. The two activities of women that are especially stressed are household work and cooking and the performance of religious observances (Murshid 1983; Chakraborty 1998). Training in gendered household work begins with the allocation of tasks like sweeping the floor, washing of utensils, clothes, etc., caring for younger siblings and learning to cook (Bagchi 1993). Girls have to help with bringing water from the well or pond for drinking, sew, make cow dung cakes, gather wood, work in the fields if needed as well as care for younger children (Cormack 1961). Girls grow up at home learning to help their mothers with the household work. They become proficient at cooking, cleaning and looking after siblings from an early age (Bagchi, Guha and Sengupta 1997).

Socialization processes and socializing institutions that turn women into gendered subjects interact and draw upon historical, religious, political and economic structures and ideologies to shape the lives of women in the socio-cultural context of Bengal. Feminine bodily norms are influenced and determined by the way in which an entire society constructs femininity and women. Gender stereotyping is seen in the games girls play, the clothes they wear and the differing notions regarding modesty and femininity. Practices based on cultural ideologies reflect not only the value attached to male members of the family, but also the ways in which female bodies are seen as needing containment, especially at puberty (Dube 1989). The notions of control and containment of the female body begins with the onset of puberty, when there is a radical change in the orientation to the body. Gender differences are highlighted even in the initiation rites performed for pubescent girls and boys, where boys are ritually introduced to the larger community, while female initiation rites involve proscription of the sexually mature female body. The growing girl is sought to be socialized into restraining her sexuality by enforcing rules of feminine comportment and ideas of decency and modesty (Das 1989). From a young age, girls learn proper attitudes and modes of behaviour, and the differing social expectations from female bodies and internalize an ideal of the body and physical appearance they needed to attract a good proposal of marriage. In arranged marriages, the examination of the prospective bride includes her physical appearance such as skin colour, hair and facial features. She is tested on her manner of speech and gait to ascertain that she did not have any deformity or disability as well as on her abilities and physical beauty (Roy 1972; Engels 1996).

Patriarchy in Bengal works in a benevolent fashion, concealing the rigid control that is exercised over the daughters and womenfolk in the family through mechanism like coercion and persuasion. The cultural strategy used is that of an image, an ideal type of a 'good' woman towards which all girls and women must aspire, or be relegated to the image of a 'bad' woman (Bandopadhyay 1995). A *bhalo meye* refers to a good girl, which in common parlance refers to a morally upright girl with all the positive feminine attributes, one who is the pivot of an ideal family. A *bhalo meye* is one who gets married and adheres to the cultural stereotype of being a wife and mother. For disabled girls, the situation is specifically different because they are not expected to get married due to the socio-cultural constructions of marriageability for women. Disabled girls, located beyond definitions of sexuality, desirability and marriageability, live in the liminal space of not being a *bhalo meye* and yet not being a maje meye or a morally bad girl.

The phase of wife and mother were the two most important phases in the life of any woman (Chakraborty 1998; Bannerji 2002). A woman's main goal in life is seen as becoming the helpmate and intelligent companion to the husband (Karlekar 1991). The national patriarchy delineated the entire space of women's cultural and social lives, with the home becoming her preserve and her functions being continuation of her husband's line and nurturing the future male progeny (Bagchi 1990, 1995). Marriage, thus, becomes central to the lives of all Bengali women (Östör and Fruzzetti 1982). Motherhood is seen as the ultimate identity for Bengali women, and is an excellent ploy to keep the women out of privileges like education and glorifying womanhood only through her reproductive powers. One of the primary responsibilities of women was seen to be rearing their children. Giving birth to a child, especially to a male child, led to an elevation of status, and as mistress of the house, women wielded power over other relations and the general household policies (Murshid 1983).

In the poorer rural and urban families, women belonging to the lower castes who worked outside their houses accepted this ideal of femininity. Women's agricultural labour was equated as assistance to their male counterparts and this double burden they carried in working with their husbands and in shouldering household work (Engels 1996). Women from the working class families helped their male relatives by feeding the domestic animals, milking the cows, husking grain and selling fish, planting and harvesting crops, etc. Thus, low class women had significant economic roles and enjoyed better status in families than women from upper class families who had no economic roles and whose educated women also didn't look for jobs (Murshid 1983). However, there is very little documentation of lives of women from poorer, rural families as most of the literature on women in Bengal is on women of middle and upper middle, upper caste families.

Notes

1. Of or relating to or characteristic of a brahmin, member of the highest of the four major castes of traditional Indian society, responsible for officiating at religious rites and studying and teaching the Vedas.
2. Literally, gentleman or well-mannered person in Bengal, referring to the new class of 'gentlefolk' who arose during colonial times (approximately 1757 to 1947). It is still used to indicate members of the upper middle and middle classes of Bengal.
3. A *bhadramahila* is a woman from the *bhadralok* class.

CHAPTER III

The Women, their Families and Social Contexts

West Bengal, a state in the eastern region of India has had a long history of rule by kings up to the twelfth century. It came under Islamic rule from the thirteenth century. Through the sixteenth century, under the Mughal rule, it developed into a wealthy centre of trade and industry. The caste system in Bengal was not very rigid and certain distinctive social traits are noticed. The hegemony of the brahminic[1] culture had been established through a careful process of incorporation of local indigenous cultural and religious symbols and traditions. The worship of local mother goddesses was promoted by transmitting its ideas through *bratas*[2] which are local tradition of religious rites performed collectively to achieve specific purposes of the Vedic religion (Bandyopadhyay 2004). European traders arrived in Bengal in the late fifteenth century and by the late eighteenth century, control of the Bengal region had passed into the hands of the British East India Company. Ever since India gained independence, West Bengal has been an important state in the Indian Union. The elected state government has changed from a right wing Congress at the time of independence to a strong leftist government, which has ruled the state from 1977 to 2011. The two districts of West Bengal covered in this study are Kolkata, an urban locale and South 24 Parganas, a district which in spite of its proximity to Kolkata still retains its rural characteristics, although there are a number of small towns to be found here too.

The Kolkata metropolis (Calcutta as it used to be known till a few years ago) is spread out on the eastern bank of river Hooghly. A district by itself, it is also the capital of West Bengal.The city forms the eastern fringes of the state and lies close to the neighbouring country, Bangladesh. The Bay of Bengalis about 60 miles away. As the East India Company established their base here, the city became the capital of British India. It quickly grew into a centre of modern education, science, culture and politics in India. The city underwent rapid industrial growth from the 1850s, especially in the textile and jute sectors. This made it necessary for the British government to develop infrastructure of the city, mostly in terms of railways and telegraph systems. The coalescence of British and Indian culture resulted in the emergence of a new class of urbane Indians, the *babus* (clerk who is literate in English).They constituted India's first middle class, and the members were mostly upper-caste Hindu professionals employed by the British rulers. Subsequently, Kolkata became a centre of the Indian independence movement and experienced widespread public agitation especially during the 1905 Partition of Bengal on communal grounds. In 1947, when India got its independence, the city became the capital of West Bengal.

According to Census of India 2011, the population of Kolkata is 4,486,679, where the total male population is 2,362,662 and the total female population is 2,124,017. However the sex ratio is quite skewed despite this being an urban centre, as there are only 899 females to 1,000 males. Although the Kolkata Municipal Corporation (KMC) is divided into 141 administrative wards, grouped into 15 boroughs, the urban agglomeration of Kolkata Metropolitan Area comprises 38 local municipalities. The suburban areas of Kolkata metropolitan district incorporate parts of the districts North 24 Parganas, South 24 Parganas, Howrah, Hooghly and Nadia. Thus, the extended metropolitan population of Kolkata is around 14 million, which makes it the third-largest urban agglomeration in India.

South 24 Parganas situated in the south-east of Kolkata is an important district of West Bengal state. With its district headquarters in Alipore, it shares the urban fringe with the metropolis on one side. The rest of the district is scattered with small towns especially near the river. Many of them serve as small ports. According to Census of India 2011, the total population of South 24 Parganas is 8,153,176, of which men are 4,182,758 and women constitute 3,970,418. The rural-urban breakup of the people living in the district is: The rural population is 1,086,220 while in the urban areas of the district, the total population is 5,820,469, and the sex ratio for the district is 949. The district is divided into five subdivisions, which have 29 blocks with 312 gram panchayats and 7 municipalities. While there are several small towns in the district, 84 per cent of the population lives in the rural areas, characterized by the lack of transport and communication facilities and weak delivery systems. According to the Census 2001, the scheduled caste comprises 39 per cent of the total population and BPL families constitute 37.21 per cent of the population. The majority of the population comprises Bengali Hindu people belonging to mahishya (lower caste agricultural labourers) caste, although there is a significant Muslim and Christian population also. Most of the land is owned by the Hindus, with the Muslims working as agricultural labourers or in the factories or industrial units located near the suburban towns. Agriculture, Industry and Pisiculture are the important economic activities mostly taken up in this district. Rice is the principal food crop grown in the area along with maize, pulses, oil seeds, potatoes and vegetables. In the district of South 24 Parganas, there are a lot of industries like the oil and jute mills.

Disabled Women Living in Rural Areas

The women living in the rural areas are from South 24 Parganas, which is part of the Gangetic delta region. It is for the most part mainly low-lying flat lands interspersed by small streams and abundant ponds. The predominant occupation in these areas is agriculture and agro-based enterprises, with most of the families that own the land growing their own paddy and meeting their annual need for rice from their harvest. The families or sometimes extended families have small landholdings, fragmented by continuous division over generations. However, as this region receives heavy rainfall and is also drained well by distributaries and streams, there are usually three harvests in a year—one in September, which is usually paddy, one in December, which may be wheat, and finally one in March which is usually vegetables or cash crops. The rice they harvest is stored for use by the family throughout the year and the excess is sold in the local markets to provide for other needs of the families. However, land distribution is skewed in most of these villages with the Hindus owning most of the agricultural land and the Muslims working as labour in these fields. On the other hand many of the small-scale village based enterprises and local businesses are owned and run by Muslim men like refashioning of clothes, refill factories, *biri*- and *muri*-making (puffed rice, made by dry roasting rice in an iron utensil). There are other kinds of economic activities in which both communities participate like nurseries and fishing, depending on their proximity either to fertile land not used for agriculture or to the river Ganges, or when it comes to finding work either in local factories or white-collar jobs in Kolkata.

The villages are located off the major roads in the area, but the *paras*[2] in which these girls are located are often the furthest from the road and can be accessed only with much difficulty. While some villages have wide paths or tracks allowing van rickshaws[3] to ply, many villages are accessible only by foot and this entails a long walk, sometimes stretching to a few kilometres to reach the home of the girls. The villages are usually divided into several *paras*, which are spatially spread out interspersed by agricultural fields, orchards and gardens and inhabited by different communities or caste groups, although some times the *para* may have a mixed community. There are a few villages with some families who are adherents of Christianity but largely the populace belongs to either Muslims or Hindus. While most of the girls belong to lower and middle class families, women from Hindu families are mostly from other backward castes like namashudras[4] and mahishyas. However, there is a healthy functional and social intermixing and dependence among all the communities with little communal tension being evident, although both communities are suspicious of each other, which is evident from the remarks made by the girls like, 'they don't eat at our feasts because they feel we may serve them beef' or 'girls in our house are not allowed to come out in front of those men'. The language spoken is Bangla although there is a different intonation given to the words in this district, which is quite distinct from the language spoken in the cities. There are also variations in the way in which different communities speak Bengali, with the Muslims using a healthy mix of Bengali and Urdu in their daily speech.

A. The Severely Disabled

SARASWATI, 26 YEARS, HINDU, SINGLE

Saraswati was born with cerebral palsy, a condition that causes her hands, legs and neck to stiffen, leading to lack of adequate control over their movements, along with speech impairment. With the help of services of a local NGO, Saraswati is now able to drag herself to a sitting position and use her hands to do the various activities of daily living like eating, dressing, etc. She can manage some of her personal care by herself, but needs help with most of her daily life activities. As she is not able to walk or even move around much by herself, she spends the day either in her wheelchair or on the veranda (raised adjoining open space in front of house) outside her room. She crawls from her room to the bathroom when she needs to and tries to attend to all her personal needs as far as possible. She spends her time at home, talking with her mother and the women living around their home. She sews and embroiders table mats provided to her by the NGO at regular intervals.

Saraswati's family comprises her parents and two brothers, while her teenaged younger sister has died a few years ago. Her family belongs to the mahishya caste, and is part of the middle class community of their village. She has never been to school, as her parents never thought of enrolling her because of her impairments. Saraswati is a happy person and loves to socialize with girls of her own age or younger. During summers she insists on being wheeled by her father to the cluster of trees in her neighbourhood where girls of the *para* meet and chat in the evenings. Saraswati feels that her mother is the main person in her life and fears the time when she will have to depend on her brothers and their wives for all support. She now regrets ill-treating her sister, who used to take a lot of care and wishes that she could return to the days of her childhood once again when life was uncomplicated.

SULEKHA, 24 YEARS, HINDU, SINGLE

Sulekha had polio when she was three years old and lost the strength in both her legs due to weakening of the muscles. As result of her mother's persistent efforts, she underwent treatment in several hospitals of Kolkata. After long periods of physiotherapy, she is now able to walk with the help of callipers on both legs and crutches. Within the house, Sulekha prefers to shuffle around holding her feet and toes with her hands. Using her hands to alternately put each leg forward, she can move very fast if she wants. Sulekha's family belongs to the lower middle class community of *Napit* or barber caste within their village. Her family includes her parents, one older brother and three other sisters, two of whom have been married off and are now living away from the family. Sulekha shares a close bond with many of her cousins and her *kaka* (father's younger brother) and *kakima* (father's younger brother's wife) who stay in the same house with them. She has studied up to Class IX after which she left her studies because she had failed in her exams. After dropping out of school two years ago, Sulekha has been receiving sewing and embroidery training from the local NGO that works with disabled people, so that in future she can set up her own tailoring business, if needed. From the time she was nine years old, Sulekha has also been working in her family business of making *muri*, initially devoting a few hours to now taking care of the work all by herself, being aided by her mother and sister. She also teams up with one of her close friends to fry some extra rice in order to earn some pocket money. She helps out during the day with some of the household work, and if her mother goes out, takes over the cooking responsibilities also. Sulekha is gruff in manner and argumentative with her family members, which has increased after the marriage of her sisters and the imminent marriage of her brother. Sulekha nurtures the secret desire to get married and have a *sansar* (commonly refers to the family household, also meaning the world) and hates the fact that she has to go on making *muri* for a living to support herself and her family.

SANDHYA, 31 YEARS, HINDU, SINGLE

Sandhya suffered a polio attack when she was two and a half years old and lost strength in both her lower limbs. At home, she sits with her legs folded under her. She crawls around with the help of her hands, dragging her legs along. She uses a tri-wheeler when she goes to work or out of the village. Sandhya lives with her sister, in a two-room house. It has a wide verandah in front and a kitchen just opposite to it. The toilets and a pond are located at the back of the house. At the age of six, Sandhya started attending the village primary school located about 500 metres away from their house. However, after completing Class V, she had to dropout because the high school was very far. As the family was in dire financial straits, Sandhya started working from home. Over the years she has been engaged in a wide variety of semi-skilled work. At present she is working in a refill factory. Seven days a week she is engaged in filling ink into plastic tubes and inserting a nib at the end to complete one refill. Sandhya visits her parents regularly to give them her salary, which they use for their food and other necessities, while her own expenses are borne by her eldest sister and brother-in-law, whom she looks upon as her guardians. Sandhya feels let down by her brothers for neglecting their parents, forcing her to leave home to work outside. She thinks that her elder sister and brother-in-law are her only support system as they have cared for her all their lives.

ASHA, 32 YEARS, HINDU, SINGLE

Asha suffered an attack of polio when she was two years old and lost all strength in her legs. Her movements have been reduced to a crawl. She is largely confined to the house and needs the help of her siblings whenever there is need to go out, mainly due to the poor condition of the village roads. Asha stays with her parents and two younger siblings, a brother and sister, as four of her younger sisters have been married off. Being Hindus from the mahishya caste, they have their own family temple, as well as an altar for the family deities. Asha's father works in a nursery and lives away from home, coming to see them once a week. Her mother mainly stays at home and takes care of all the household work in addition to making shoe-brushes to supplement the family income. She does not allow her daughters to do any household work though they belong to the middle class category in their village. Asha's extended family of paternal uncles and second cousins, live in and around their home, providing support to each other in times of need. At the age of six, Asha was admitted to the village primary school, but dropped out as she reached secondary school. This was because the nearest high school was in Bankrahat, six kilometres from her house. Since then, from the age of thirteen, Asha has been making *biris* at home contributing her earnings to the family finances. She has also learnt embroidery and gets work from the local businessmen for embroidering sarees and dress materials. Recently she has completed a training course in *ari* (embroidery work with sequins and stones) from an NGO for disabled women. With their support she has started doing specialized embroidery considerably increasing her monthly income. Now both she and her youngest sister embroider sarees, while her brother works part time in a nursery to support his studies. Presently Asha is happy with life, surrounded by siblings who love and care for her. However, she fears the day when they would be married and may not have enough time for her. They would not be able to help her move about the village whenever she wants.

B. The Moderately Disabled

RITA, 34 YEARS, HINDU, SINGLE

Rita had polio when she was 18 months old and ever since has been walking with a pronounced limp or with the help of callipers. The muscles of both her legs were weakened but more so the left leg. At home Rita doesn't use her callipers, preferring to walk about with a shaky gait supporting her left leg with one hand. She finds it very difficult to manage her daily life with callipers on. Moreover, her knee joints have been fixed through surgery so she cannot fold her legs. This causes problems at every stage as most work in the village requires one to squat on the floor. Rita's family belongs to the lower middle class group within their village. She is of the mahishya caste and her family comprises her parents, her two married brothers and their families. Rita's father is too old to work in the fields and has handed over most of their lands to her elder brother to cultivate. Her younger brother has received a small plot of land on which he has started a paan (betel leaf) vine, which he hopes will bring him a steady income in the coming years. Rita's home has two parts; on one side are three *kaccha* (not cemented, made of bamboo, hay and mud) rooms in which her brothers and their families live while across the courtyard, are the two *pucca* (cemented) rooms, in which Rita and her parents live. They use the courtyard or the open verandahs for cooking on the mud and clay ovens built here. Rita has studied up to Class XII, and completed a four-month long secretarial training programme in Punjab. But due to lack of opportunity, she is now at home, supporting herself and her mother by embroidering on sarees, stitching clothes and making paper packets.

SALEMA, 30 YEARS, MUSLIM, MARRIED

Salema became disabled as a result of an injection administered during an illness when she was two. She has never regained the full strength of her left leg and continues to walk with a slight limp. Additionally, an eye infection at around the age of eight has left her vision partially impaired. Due to financial constraints, she never went to school, but started working at a very young age. She washed and ironed the clothes that her brothers stitched to provide for the family. Presently, Salema lives with her visually impaired husband and three children in her in-laws' house. Salema got married to Yusuf ten years ago, through a proposal brought by common family friends. Her husband's brothers live next door and her *sasuri* (mother-in-law) helps Salema with the household work, if she is busy with the ironing of clothes. Salema's husband, runs a teashop in another *para* (locality) of the village, while she irons clothes as part of the main business of the village. They belong to the lower class group in their village and somehow manage to sustain themselves on their combined earnings.

C. The Mildly Disabled

JAHANARA, 34 YEARS, MUSLIM, MARRIED

She lives with her husband, three children, her mother-in-law and two brothers-in-law. Jahanara's disability is mild, as only one leg is affected, which causes difficulties in walking and slows her down while going about the household chores. When she was 18 months old, Jahanara developed a boil on her right leg that needed to be drained. The local doctor pierced a nerve in the process, permanently damaging a muscle in her right leg. This resulted in the under-development of her right leg making her walk with a slight limp. Her limp becomes especially visible when she walks fast on the rough beaten track to their house. Jahanara is the sixth of ten siblings and her parental home is in the Hooghly district of West Bengal. She has studied up to middle school but was forced to drop out of school by her father when she was in class VII. It was a time of political violence in the area and he felt it was dangerous for a girl to go out of the house. Jahanara got married four years after she left school to a groom fixed by her *mama* (maternal uncle). Jahanara has now been married for 11 years and is living with her in-laws in the house on her husband's ancestral property.

APARNA, 30 YEARS, HINDU, MARRIED

She lives with her husband, daughter, mother-in-law and sister-in-law in a village in the Falta block of South 24 Parganas. Aparna had polio when she was six months old resulting in a weak left leg. In time her left foot has developed a bony deformity that gets painful when she puts her weight on it. It also gives rise to recurrent sores. Now Aparna walks with a pronounced limp, sometimes with one hand on her knee for support as her left foot is very thin and also bent inwards. When she puts her full weight on it, the ankle bones hurt. Aparna's natal family consisted of her parents and six daughters, of whom Aparna was the oldest. Aparna's father used to make *biris* or work as a labourer in the agricultural season. Because of poor financial conditions she never attended school and from an early age started helping in the *biri* binding process along with the other family members. Aparna's father died when she was 16 years old and she became the main breadwinner in their family. She has to shoulder the responsibility of all her sisters. Aparna herself married four years ago having met her husband, who lived in the same village, through her father's *biri* business. Her family belongs to the Namoshudra caste and to the lower class group in their village. Aparna and her husband make *biris* for a living, although Aparna also works as a labour during the agricultural season in order to supplement their family income. But for her daughter, Aparna finds her married life unbearable.

MITA, 38 YEARS, HINDU, SINGLE

Mita lives in a village, around three kilometres away from Canning town, which serves as a link for boats and steamers for going to the Sunderbans. Mita was affected by polio when she was nine months old and as a result, has reduced strength in her left leg, from hip to toe. She walks with a pronounced limp and has an ankle length calliper that she wears occasionally while going out. Mita's family belongs to the baidya (high-caste Hindu community, ranking next to brahmins but above kayasthas of Bengal) caste but her father had started a business of buying and selling rice. Mita is the fourth among seven siblings; three of her sisters, two older and one younger have been married off, while Mita and her second sister are unmarried. Mita's father passed away in 1998. Her family now consists of her mother, two brothers, a sister-in-law and a niece and another single sister. Mita's second sister, who works for an NGO in Birbhum district, has been supporting the family for the last 15 years. Mita's brothers own a shop that sells steel products in the town. Their family belongs to the upper middle class group of their community. Mita completed her Bachelor of Art by supporting herself through money earned from tuitions. After her graduation, she got a job with an NGO working for disabled children, as supervisor of the residential children's home. She worked there for 10 years before resigning. Presently she is enjoying her family life and considering her future career options. Her experience makes her feel that disabled women like her should never dream of a life that non-disabled women enjoy in society.

ANITA, 27 YEARS, HINDU, SINGLE

Anita lives in a village in Diamond Harbour block II, at a distance of about 65 km. from Kolkata. She was born with dwarfism, a congenital condition characterized by short stature (about 3 ft. tall) and associated orthopaedic problems like short limbs and a large head. At the time of her birth this condition manifested itself through short thin limbs. Anita couldn't move by herself till she was three years old, nor was she able to use her limbs, even for tasks like eating. Anita learnt to sit with support, started walking at around five years of age and learnt to talk even later. She is the youngest of ten siblings with six brothers and three sisters, all of whom have been married off. Anita lives with her parents and married brothers in a home spread over two buildings connected by a pond that lies in between.

Anita started going to the village primary school, which is about one kilometre away from her home, when she was around eight years old, but as she found it difficult to remember what she learnt, she dropped out of school after remaining in the same class for many years. When she was 16 years old, she enrolled for adult literacy classes run in her village. She has now learnt to sign her name, read and write, and do simple mathematical calculations and deal with money. Earlier she had worked in a hotel, performed in a circus and done odd jobs in the cement factory near her home. After remaining unemployed for some time, Anita has recently undergone a *zari* (embroidery using golden thread) and *ari* training from an NGO working for disabled women about 20 km. away from her house. Anita is a happy person and very optimistic about her life, though she fears that in future her *mejda* (second elder brother) who is looking after her now, may not do so as he sees his other brothers ignoring her presence.

Disabled Women Living in Urban Areas

Of the women living in the urban areas, three live in a residential institution in south-eastern part of Kolkata, one is married and living with her family in the south-western part of the city and one lives by herself away from her family because of her work. These women live in densely populated neighbourhoods of Kolkata, where there are people from different religious, socio-cultural and economic backgrounds. There is interaction with the neighbours, but on a more neutral basis than in the villages where the neighbours form part of the extended family. Of the three girls living in the residential institution, two have grown up in family set up while Dora has lived here from her early childhood. Among the women living in the urban sprawl, two of the girls belong to trading families, while the others come from families that were in salaried jobs. The women come mostly from the middle class, and belong to upper castes (brahmins and baidyas) and middle castes (baishyas), while two belong to the Christian community.

A. The Severely Disabled

DORA, 37 YEARS, CHRISTIAN, SINGLE

Dora has lived in a residential institution for disabled women in south Kolkata from the time she was around two years old. She was born with cerebral palsy as a result of contracting jaundice while in her mother's womb. When she was one year old, Dora's mother left her father and her, as she could not cope with the demands of a disabled child. Dora was shifted to the home when she was two years old, as her father couldn't take proper care of her properly at home. Dora's father has been the steady presence in her life and comes to meet her once a month. Her disabilities involve lack of adequate control over her hands, legs and spine and minor speech impairment. She uses a wheelchair for moving around and is able to grasp things with an unsteady hand. Since the age of six, Dora has been attending a special school/institute for people with cerebral palsy located at a distance of about 15 km. from the home. She was taught subjects like mathematics and science, but because of a very poor memory, Dora could not proceed in formal school education. Presently she is attending classes at the National Open School, hoping to pass the Class X exams. Dora had completed a cooking and bakery course, after which she had hoped to start her own business. However, the responsibilities involved in running a bakery was something she could not cope with. She then did an informal course in computers at the NGO and hopes to find a job in some computer related field. She sometimes works as a translator and interpreter for her disabled friends who give lectures in different seminars and workshops. She also helps them to prepare the script for the lecture and types it for them. Dora also works with a disabled adults' advocacy group to spread awareness regarding the status of the disabled people in society through mono-acts, plays and songs.

CHOBI, 31 YEARS, HINDU, SINGLE

Chobi has been living at the residential institution ever since the death of her father four years ago. She is the only daughter of her parents and the only child in their entire family. When she was three years old, she was dually attacked by typhoid and measles leaving her partially paralysed from neck downwards. She has very little sensation or strength in her limbs. Flexibility and strength of her joints are also restricted allowing her only a limited control over her hands. She can hold big things but cannot manage fine-tuned movements as a result of which she needs help with all her daily activities. She has a sharp brain with very clear speech, and can recount minute details of her life at home. Chobi's family, belonging to the brahmin caste, owns a flat on the fourth floor of a building in north Kolkata, where she lived with her parents and grandparents. As a result of her prolonged illness and its paralytic effect on her, Chobi's parents never thought of sending her to school or to any special institution. Though there were only a few special schools at that time, there was a government run one near their home. After the sudden demise of her father, Chobi's mother, fearing that she would be unable to cope single handed, decided to shift her to this Home. Her mother has donated a lump sum to the management to ensure that she is well cared for as long as she lives.

AGATHA, 34 YEARS, CHRISTIAN, SINGLE

Agatha lives in a busy upper middle class locality of central Kolkata. An area which has some of the earliest settlement of the city. She was born with a medical condition called arthrogryposis with spina bifida, that gave her stiff joints and bones. This to a great extent affected her ability to stand and walk. After a series of surgeries, Agatha can now walk with waist length callipers and crutches with belts at the hips, knees and ankles. However, at home she prefers to use a wheelchair or just her crutches. Agatha started school when she was four years old, and went through painful experiences in two different schools before being admitted to a well-known school in central Kolkata, from where she completed her schooling. Agatha completed her M.A. from a university in New Delhi and came back to work in Kolkata with a leading NGO, first in the rural areas and then in their urban programme. At present, after completing her B.Ed. degree, Agatha is a primary teacher at a reputed convent school of Kolkata. She also volunteers in an NGO that provides extra coaching in school subjects to slum children as well as financing their education and other related needs.

SMITA, 36 YEARS, HINDU, SINGLE

Smita lives in the same residential institution as Dora, but has been there only for the last eight years. She had encephalitis when she was three years old and was left with residual physical damage that affected her legs and speech. Smita's family, which had migrated from Midnapore district, used to live in south Kolkata in a small room with shared bathrooms and open kitchen space on the ground floor. Smita lived there with her parents and four younger siblings—two sisters and two brothers. Her father used to work as a peon in an office nearby and her lower middle class family belongs to the mahishya caste. Her parents never thought of sending her to school, although all her younger siblings were admitted to the municipal school nearest to their house. When she was about 7–8 years old, she was admitted to the newly opened school for disabled children, where she underwent physical therapy and also received educational support (remedial functional education, using techniques that stimulate mental ability but help disabled person to progress at their own pace). Since then Smita has been associated with the institute. Initially she received academic training and later different vocational trainings—like batik, tie and dye, painting and clay modelling, and finally cooking and baking. Presently Smita is training supervisor of the catering unit at the institute where she received training. She moves in a wheelchair around her place of work and by crawling within the residential institution, which is now her home. Smita's family has moved back to their natal village in Midnapore district after her father retired from his job. Smita wants to lead an independent life. After eight years of living at the Home, though in regular contact with her family she wants a room of her own.

B. The Moderately Disabled

MANJU, 40 YEARS, HINDU, MARRIED

Manju lives with her husband and son in the south-western fringes of Kolkata, near her natal home. She had polio when she was three years old, resulting in a weakened right leg. At home she walks with a pronounced limp or with a hand to support her knee, but outside, she wears a calliper in order to walk properly. Belonging to a family of the baishya caste, Manju was the last but one of six siblings. Her two sisters are married and her elder brother lives with his wife's family because of property disputes. Her younger brother has constructed and shifted to his own house down the road. Manju's parents and a married brother live in her natal home across the road from her house while her eldest brother has constructed his own home at a distance and moved away. Manju completed her graduation and has been working for over 18 years as a steno-typist in a business house in the city. She got married 16 years

TABLE 3.1: Summary Information of the Research Participants

	Name	*Age*	*Location*	*Marital status*	*Disability*	*Employed/ Unemployed*
MILD DISABILITY						
1	Jahanara	34	Rural	Married	Polio right leg, walks with a slight limp	housewife
2	Aparna	30	Rural	Married	Polio left leg, foot bent inward	makes *biris* at home
3	Anita	27	Rural	Single	Short stature, associated orthopaedic problems	looking for employment
4	Mita	38	Rural	Single	Polio right leg, walks with a slight limp	recently quit job in NGO
MODERATE DISABILITY						
5	Manju	40	Urban	Married	Polio left leg, uses callipers while going out	works in an office as typist
6	Krishna	40	Urban	Widowed	Polio right leg, walks with a limp, uses callipers always	working in a NGO
7	Rita	34	Rural	Single	Polio right leg, walks with a slight limp, uses callipers	does embroidery at home
8	Salema	30	Rural	Married	Polio left leg, walks with a slight limp, one eye vision impaired	sewing and ironing of altered clothing
SEVERE DISABILITY						
9	Asha	32	Rural	Single	Polio both legs, moves by crawling	does embroidery at home
10	Sandhya	31	Rural	Single	Polio both legs, moves on the backside, uses tricycle	works in a refill factory
11	Sulekha	24	Rural	Single	Polio both legs, moves on her backside, uses callipers	makes *muri* at home
12	Saraswati	26	Rural	Single	Cerebral Palsy, wheelchair user, movements of all limbs restricted	not employed, speech severely affected
13	Chobi	31	Urban	Single	Cerebral Palsy, all limbs affected, wheelchair user	not employed

(*Contd.*)

TABLE 3.1 (*contd.*)

	Name	*Age*	*Location*	*Marital status*	*Disability*	*Employed/ Unemployed*
14	Dora	37	Urban	Single	Cerebral Palsy, wheelchair user	still studying, works as interpreter
15	Smita	36	Urban	Single	Cerebral Palsy, both legs and spine badly affected, moves by crawling	working in a NGO
16	Agatha	34	Urban	Single	Arthogryposis, legs and spine more affected, uses callipers/wheelchair	teaches in secondary school

ago and started living with her husband near her in-laws' home. Her husband is an artisan and makes handicraft items to sell in fairs and shops and now has a thriving business. They moved to a place near her parents' home so that her mother could take care of the child when she went to work. Not only is it closer to her workplace, but her husband's business also got a boost because of their move to the city. Manju's son is completing his graduation and all three of them keep busy in their respective schedules, with the responsibility for housework resting mainly on Manju's shoulders. They now have a comfortable lifestyle and are in the upper middle class category.

KRISHNA, 40 YEARS, HINDU, WIDOWED

Krishna runs an NGO for disabled women and children in the rural areas of South 24 Parganas. In Kolkata, Krishna's natal house is in a busy locality in the north, with a lot of traffic in front of their two-storied house. When she was two years old Krishna was affected by polio and was fitted with a calliper on one leg. Now she uses an extra light calliper on her left leg whenever she goes out but at home, she walks with a slight limp or sometimes with a hand to support her left knee. Krishna belongs to a kayastha (a caste or community of Hindus working as record-keepers and administrators of the state) family, comprising her parents and two brothers. Her father had a printing business which is now being run by her brothers, who are married and have families. Krishna studied in mainstream schools and was doing a course in homeopathic medicine, when she met her husband. Despite opposition from his family, they decided to get married while she was still in college. Within a few months of her marriage, her husband suffered a massive heart attack and passed away. Since then, Krishna tried her hand at different jobs, from practising medicine, to working at a secretarial job in an arts and drama centre, to being associated, first with the women's rights movement and finally with the disability movement. After working for a few years in different NGOs, Krishna decided to set up her own NGO, which works for the empowerment of women with disabilities in rural areas. She lives in the organization's office that operates out of one of the villages in which they are working in the Falta block, about 45 km. from Kolkata. Her NGO is trying to organize disabled women into self-help groups as well as mobilizing them to rally for better utilization of government schemes and programmes.

Notes

1. Religious practices symbolizing devotion to any deity, usually performed by women in Bengal.
2. Neighbourhood, cluster of houses, may vary in size from a few houses to the entire village or area.
3. The van rickshaw, which is a popular mode of transport in rural Bengal, is an open cart with three wheels, with a cycle type handle in front. While the van puller sits in the front and pedals, the passengers sit at the back. At a time the van may accommodate 4-5 adults. This is a cheap and popular mode of transport in rural areas as they can go into the smallest alleys and need low investment.
4. The Namashudras also known as the Chandals or lowest caste of Bengal, lived mainly in the eastern districts of Bengal, but after independence when these areas were ceded to Bangladesh, the inhabitants were forced to migrate across to West Bengal.

CHAPTER IV

Not a *Bhalo Meye*
Constructing Differences

While I was growing up, I desperately wanted to be normal like all others.

Gender socialization is one of the basic processes whereby identities are constructed and maintained through learning of socio-cultural ideologies regarding appropriate behaviour and practices and its performance and practice in daily life contexts. It is evident that all girls, disabled or not, are socialized into gender identities; but for disabled girls, the socialization process is tempered by the way in which their impairments are interpreted within their families and in the context in which they are located. Bengali gender culture that attributes the essence of womanhood as being a wife and mother, treats the disabled girl benevolently, almost as if compensating for the girl's inability to attain and achieve such socially valued roles. Parents' reaction to the onset of disability reflects the way in which women are constructed as potentially productive and reproductive beings, which spurs them to seek measures that will restore the girl to minimum standards of normality.

This chapter explores the childhood experiences of disabled girls and the ways in which they are socialized within their families and by the community around them. The aim is to highlight the varied processes through which these girls learn to accept and live according to gendered/disabled norms that govern their entire lives and lead to the creation of differences that underpin their identity. The first section looks at the initial responses to the impairment of a daughter within the family and the ways in which families and communities dealt with the onset of disability. The chapter brings to light the ways in which disabled daughters, perceived by the socio-cultural ideologies as imperfect and flawed, are loved and cared for, and socialized into gendered/disabled identities, with startling similarities and subtle differences created and reinforced between them and their brothers and sisters. The chapter seeks to understand the subtle and apparent ways in which differences were created between the disabled girl and her other siblings, the ways in which impairment of the girl is reconciled to the imperatives of her gendered socialization and the socio-cultural processes that construct her femininity and disability in ways that are different from that of other women around her. The second section highlights the process of creation of difference within the family and in the wider social networks a disabled girl is part of and her own responses to it.

'Why Me?' Responses to a Disabled Girl

Asch (2001) stresses that identity, essentialism and community take on a particular significance when we remember that disability, unlike race or sex, is not usually shared by the members of one's biological or social family. Broadly speaking, parents and siblings of disabled children usually have rarely encountered people with such conditions in their lives. Hence, the incidence of disability or a visible impairment in a daughter in a socio-cultural milieu that focuses on the productive and reproductive capacities of the woman evinces varying reactions from parents and families. Parents experience shock, anxiety, helplessness and react by questioning as to why this happened to them. The visual impact of the disability of the child, the severity of disability and the birth order of the child coupled with the reactions of relatives and neighbours have an impact on the shock experienced by the parents and the family. Only when the girl starts growing up do the parents and the girl herself start realizing the nature and extent of the impact of the impairment on the daily life of the girl, and the ways in which it affects the family.

Anita, born with congenital problems, was a tiny, underweight baby with short, thin and crooked arms and legs. When Anita's mother was lamenting the condition of her baby, their neighbours and other family members were loudly speculating the fact that a 'deformed' child had been born to a woman who had already given birth to nine 'normal' children. Some of the neighbours also advised her to throw away the infant, but she refused, willing to care for and rear her 'grotesque' baby daughter as best as she could. Agatha's mother was shocked when the doctors at the hospital told her that her new born daughter was severely disabled and would not be able to move around by herself. 'They said that she would be less intelligent, would not be able to do anything, would not be able to move at all.' But she recalls that there were no doubts expressed by either her husband or his parents about Agatha and her place in their family. When Saraswati, the eldest child of her parents, was born with cerebral palsy, her mother was both shocked and worried as some of the village people cast aspersions on her ability to bear 'normal' children. At that time, as they had no idea about the exact nature of her limitations, her parents were determined to ensure that their daughter would be loved and cared for in the family.

Although there is acceptance and love for the disabled daughter born into the family, especially by mothers, Dora's experience was unusual in that she was rejected by her mother. She was born in a nursing home in Kolkata with congenital disabilities, having contracted jaundice in her mother's womb. According to Dora's father, her mother, unable to cope with the fact that her first child was disabled, left her in her father's care when she was six months old and moved away to another city. Dora has grown up feeling that her mother had deserted her, as she could not cope with a visibly flawed daughter. 'My mother might have thought that I would be a vegetable all my life, and so she left me. If I had been normal, she wouldn't have thrown me away like this. How could she throw me out because I am not normal?'

Parents of girls afflicted by polio or diseases like typhoid and encephalitis, realized the impact of the impairment only after the associated symptoms of high fever lessened and their daughters were left with paralysed limbs and associated impairments. In the villages, superstitions and religious beliefs, which reflect the socio-cultural ideologies regarding disabled people, are used as a means of rationalizing and explaining the 'tragedy' that caused the impairment. One common belief is that the disabling illness was caused by the touch of a menstruating woman, who is considered to be highly polluting and harmful. Aparna says that her mother believed that she became disabled as a menstruating woman touched her during high fever. 'They say that if *asuti* (unclean) women who are in their menstruation cycle touch you, then you become paralysed. My mother is sure that some woman having her menses must have touched me.' Asha's mother also feels that 'an *asuti* woman must have touched her during her measles.' Supernatural reasons are also cited for onset of disability, ranging from *tuktak* (black magic) to the influence of ghosts, to punishment for sins. Rita's mother said that the village people believed that Rita's illness and her subsequent disability were caused by a '*bhoot*' (ghost) or '*pretatma*' (evil spirit). Another major view is that the disability is the result of the sins committed either by them or their family members. Mita as a toddler had walked into a cyclonic storm on Saraswati Puja[1] day, and had contracted the high fever, which resulted in her disability. Mita's mother believes that Mita's disability was caused by divine anger over sins committed by her.

However, within a few weeks, the initial shock experienced by the parents and family is overtaken by concern for the girl and an urge to ensure that the impairment is cured or its impact lessened so that the girl will be able to lead a life as 'normal' as possible. Parents seek to legitimize the impairment and represent it as *asukh* or illness and believe that it can be cured. Representing disability as an *asukh* is a mechanism used by many parents who find it easy to justify the disability of their daughter to the outside world and even to themselves. If disability is considered to be an *asukh* then there is hope for a miraculous cure to restore her to normalcy. Chobi remembers that her parents would always refer to her condition as an illness, whenever people outside the family asked about her.

Guided by religious beliefs, parents explored indigenous systems in search for a 'cure' for their daughter. The paramount fear, especially in minds of the mothers, was that as a girl, in a gendered socio-cultural context, 'she would have to be able to take care at least of herself, if not of the other members of the family'. In the gendered culture of Bengal, as women's primary roles are of wife and mother, they have to be capable of doing household work. Girls have the responsibility of maintaining the *sansar* once they grow up. Saraswati's mother opined, 'Who will feed a woman just like that if she is not able to work?' In a gender regime where mothers are responsible for the training of their daughters for their future roles, the onset of disability is seen as a catastrophe for the young daughter who becomes flawed and physically less capable than all other girls. Perceiving that their disabled daughters would have to struggle against a social order that values women's productive and reproductive capabilities, mothers sought 'cures' through prayers offered at different shrines, consulting sadhus (godmen) and faith healers to ensure that their girl was least affected by the disability. Large amounts of money were spent on visiting several sadhus and *tantriks* (local healers using powerful ritual acts of body, speech, and mind) in search of a cure, using balms and oil for massage and special pujas or worship for her well-being. Asha recalls that whenever her mother would hear of a new sadhu coming to their locality, she would immediately take her to him asking for blessings and hoping for a remedy that would make her get better. Saraswati's mother took her to a *pirsthan* (Muslim secular place of pilgrimage) in Ghutiari Sharif (about 60 km. from their village), where they first anointed her body with blessed oil and then dipped her in the holy pond nearby, so that she would get better. Sandhya's parents used to take her to *kavirajs* (Ayurvedic doctors) and *thans* (Hindu religious shrines) as well as to sadhus.

When indigenous belief systems failed to restore their daughter to 'normal', parents opted for medical treatment in the hope of improving her condition and reducing the visible impact of the disability. Agatha's parents took her to different specialist doctors and hospitals to ensure that she would be able to walk. She underwent a series of surgeries, and by the time she was 4 years old, was able to walk with the help of crutches and callipers. Agatha's mother feels that at that time their only concern was 'that she would at least be able to walk a little'. Parents hoped that reducing the visual impact of the disability would give a semblance of normalcy and would also enable their daughter to be more independent. To this purpose, the main thrust was put on being able to walk, with the assumption that it would enable their disabled daughter to lead a life as 'normal' as possible, so that she would be able to fulfil her designated roles within the family set-up. Agatha now says, 'It was so important for my parents and even for me that I should be able to walk. When I used to see the other children walking about and playing, I wondered why I couldn't do so, too?'

Parents undertook many tiring and expensive trips to hospitals in Kolkata, which included travelling far and for long hours, mobilizing funds and companions to escort them as well as arranging care for their other children. Sulekha's grandfather would escort her and her mother to the hospital every time as her father was busy managing their family business of making *muri*. Her village was not well connected with the city at that time and to go to the hospital meant leaving at 4 in the morning with the trucks carrying *muri* and returning late in the evening. 'It used to be quite expensive as we sometimes had to pay a van rickshaw to bring us back into the village from the main town in Amtala. At that time, our finances were quite strained.' The support of other members of the family and even neighbours was solicited for taking care of other children or for accompanying the mothers and the disabled daughters in case any male member of the family was unavailable as escort. Asha's grandmother used to take care of her younger sisters every time she had to go to the hospital. Saraswati's mother said, 'In those days village women hardly went outside their villages. Whenever I had to take my daughter to the hospital in Kolkata, I had to ask her father to come with me. If he couldn't then her grandfather, maternal or paternal uncles would accompany me.' Jahanara's and Aparna's mothers would enlist the help of their neighbours in the village to take them to the hospital for treatment. In Kolkata, Manju's parents engaged a local unemployed man to take her to the hospital every week, learn and administer the exercises prescribed for her.

However, protective fathers and concerned mothers were wary of the impact of medical treatment on their daughter, and mindful of the pain she had to suffer during the process of rehabilitation. The love and concern acted as a deterrent both in accessing services and in continuing with the rehabilitation process. Agatha recalls that her soft-hearted father was appalled by the scars of her surgeries and wanted to discontinue it in order to save her from more pain. When Manju was first taken to the hospital, the doctors wanted to operate on her to restore more strength to her legs; but at that time, her parents refused to let them operate, as they had never heard of such treatment succeeding and feared that her condition would worsen. Jahanara's *baba* (father) and *ma* (mother) were very worried when the doctor wanted to operate on her leg to correct the defect. 'Initially *baba* wanted the operation as he had anticipated problems at the time of my marriage, but when the doctor said that he couldn't guarantee full recovery of power in my leg, *baba* was unwilling to take the chance. He was thankful that at least I could walk and as a girl who would have to be married off, I needed to be as normal as possible.' When a medical camp was organized in her village, Aparna's father refused to take her there, as he was afraid that surgery would take away the little strength she had in her disabled leg. 'Father didn't give any importance to it.'

Mothers: Primary caregivers of the disabled daughter

Gilligan (1982) posited that women have a personality that is oriented towards relationships permitting them to evince greater empathy than men and, thus, to assume caring roles within the family and society. The gender culture in Bengal assigns all responsibility for bearing, care and rearing of children, especially in the formative years to mothers, who are constructed and idealized as 'natural' carers, while fathers are the breadwinners of the family. For disabled girls, needing additional care and support, the ideology is reinforced and mothers become the primary carers. Saraswati's father expressed, 'After all it is a woman's work to care for the child. I am working outside the house and how long am I at home? At most I can bring the water for her bath. Her mother had to do more for her. That's her duty.' While most parents accepted that it was the mother's responsibility to care for the disabled daughter, staff of non-government organizations working with the disabled reinforced notions of gendered care. In her childhood, her mother had been forced to leave Saraswati with her maternal grandparents who lived in the same village, as she could not manage all the household tasks, caring for the other children and tending to Saraswati's every need. However, the NGO staff insisted on teaching Saraswati's mother the physiotherapy exercises, and she had to go every day to administer the therapy to her child. When she protested that it was her sisters and mother who took care of Saraswati on a daily basis, she was told that she should pay more attention to her disabled child. When Saraswati moved back to her father's house she was around 12 years old, her mother took over the entire responsibility for her care, from bathing, dressing, toileting, feeding as well as doing the exercises, while managing to devote equal time to all her other household responsibilities.

Agatha's mother gave up her job to care for her, which involved both physically caring for her as well as taking her to medical and paramedical professionals so that she would be able to walk. When she would be admitted into hospital for surgery, her mother stayed with her there, and when she needed to go for follow up visits once a week, it was again her mother who accompanied her, as her father was working hard, 'to provide for the family as well as for the treatment'. Chobi's father used to stay away from home for work and would come home only once a month or when she needed to be taken to the doctor for regular checkups. She remembers her mother as her primary caregiver, attending to all her daily needs from helping her with her toileting and cleaning needs, bathing and dressing her and feeding her as well as attending to the household chores and to the needs of her aging grandparents. The carer role played by the mother from the formative days has implications for girls with disabilities in their adulthood, where they find their mothers as sole friends, once the other girls in the family marry and leave the family home.

Women, who cannot or are not able to care for their disabled child, are termed as 'bad women' as they do not adhere to or follow the stereotypical labels of mother attached to them. Dora's mother left her and her father and moved to another city when Dora was six months old. Dora feels that it was her disability that caused her mother to 'dump' them both and blames her for deserting her. 'If I had not been like this would she have left me? She didn't leave my other siblings.' Although her father almost immediately arranged for Dora to be shifted into a residential home, Dora feels that despite being a father, he tried his best to provide for her care and attempts to justify his reasons for institutionalizing her. 'I needed a lot of care while I was an infant and to care for me, my father would have to work from home, so that he did not have to leave me with strangers or with babysitters. So he was forced to send me here to the Home.' She recalls that she was provided with good care at the Home and even though she missed her parents, she lived there comfortably.

When fathers participate in care responsibilities, they are praised and looked up to for engaging in work that is not considered by gender culture ideologies as apt for them. Chobi looks upon her father fondly and remembers that whenever her father would come home or her mother fell ill, he would take over some of the work relating to her daily care from her mother. 'He was capable of taking care of me single-handedly, helping with everything from toileting, bathing, dressing to feeding. When *baba* was around, he would look after me all through the day to give *ma* some rest.' Mita recalls that although her mother used to accompany her to the hospital as her father had to run his business, every evening he would sit with her to do the physiotherapy exercises and massage her legs with oil. She feels grateful that he made time for her, even though caring for her was not one of his socially assigned family responsibilities.

Thus, the disabled girl finds herself located in a scenario where parents, family members and neighbours, although disappointed and dismayed by the onset of disability, either at birth or later, accept and come to love the little girl along with her impairment. The main fear of all parents is that the child would not be able to cope with the demands that are made on girls, especially in a male-dominated society. Hence, they attempt to counteract the impact of the impairment on the girl and restore her to the so-called norms of a 'normal' body by seeking different kinds of treatment, whether belonging to indigenous belief systems or to medical and therapeutic systems. The imperative towards attaining normal bodily standards ensured that parents used whatever resources were available at their disposal to enable their daughter to counter the consequences of their impairments. Mothers emerge as the main support system in this process, probably because they realize the implications of being a woman more so than any male member of the family. Mothers were not only the primary carers but also the inspiration throughout the painful processes of rehabilitation undergone by most of these women. Fathers assume a secondary role in the early childhood period and emerge as strong influences in late childhood, as gender ideologies of Bengal represent the father-daughter relationship as one of close bonding and companionship.

Growing up: Developing Gendered/Disabled Identities

Within the family, disabled girls live a protected and pampered life, cared for by their mothers and sisters and cosseted by their fathers and other extended family members. They forge close bonds with their siblings and cousins staying nearby and in childhood participate in family and community activities like other children do. The disabled girl is treated with a lot of affection and care, as most daughters are often treated at home in their childhood, and sometimes with more concern and protectiveness than the other children in the family. Differences are created subtly between them and their siblings—differences which are not always negative or discriminatory but seem to reinforce her special status in the family. These creation of differences are based on perceptions about their impairments, pain associated with their impairments and their medical rehabilitation, associated insufficiencies, both actual and constructed, which are linked to the construction and performance of gendered abilities. Such processes of socialization serve to concretize and consolidate the gender identity of disabled girls, while at the same time, underline her distinctiveness and mark her as different from the other children around her.

'Onyoder moton noy to' (Not like others): Creating Differences

Parents, in their efforts to provide their disabled daughter with a cushioned existence, created a distinct difference between her and her other siblings by granting special privileges, pampering her and excusing the girl from household chores. Although the degree of disability influenced such actions to a great extent, parental cosseting reveals the nature of the socio-cultural ideologies that construct the disabled girl as weak and in need of protection. Girls remember their fathers as especially indulgent, from giving them extra pocket money to being anxious whenever they suffered pain because of their impairments. Jahanara's father, who was very stern and strict with all his other children, never used to scold her for the extra favours she took from him.

'*Abba* (father) always used to have change in his pocket and only I among all siblings was allowed to go and take money out from there whenever I wished. If I asked him for bigger amounts of money he never said no. But to my other siblings he would give only fixed and small amounts of money.' Chobi recounts that her parents used to argue over disciplining her. 'If *ma* scolded me, *baba* used to scold *ma*. Ma occasionally got angry with me as I would make her run around doing odd jobs in addition to all her *sansarer kaaj*.[14] *Baba* used to tell her not to scold me.'

Aparna's *baba* was fiercely protective of her at home and never allowed her to do any *sansarer kaaj*. 'Even if anyone asked me to, he would scold my mother and sisters and say "so many of you are there, can't you manage?" He felt that because I was disabled I wouldn't be able to do the work. As long as my *baba* was alive, I was never allowed to do much of the household work.' Mita's parents and even her elder sisters would hardly let her do any of the household work that was considered as heavy work. 'If I went to fetch water sometimes *ma* would say you don't have to go, you will have problems. They never let me do any of the outside work like going to the shops or the market or even drawing water from the pond or tap. *Ma* always used to say "how can she do it? With so many siblings around why should she have to go out at all?"' When Asha found it difficult to walk on the rough village paths with callipers and crutches, her father advised her to stop wearing the mobility aids, as 'Baba couldn't bear to see me cry. He would say, "let it be, if she is going to cry so much she needn't wear it".' In Sandhya's home, when her elder sister used to insist on her wearing the calliper everyday, her father, seeing her in pain, asked her to wear it only at home. 'As he couldn't bear the pain I was in, he told me, "if you want to wear them then do so, if you don't that is also ok".'

From childhood, siblings are also made to realize and accept that their sister is special and needs extra support and help from them. Agatha's siblings took care to include her in their games, but she recalls that 'it was explained to them that I would need extra care'. Sisters become the main support system in childhood or till they are able to manage their personal care by themselves, helping them with their care tasks and providing them with company. Asha recalls that it was her younger sisters who assisted her in all the daily living activities, from taking bath to going to the toilet. 'My sisters would carry my clothes to the pond . . . wash and put my clothes for drying...wash my plate after I finished eating . . . and also encourage me to go with them to play.' In her teenage years, as their mother was busy with *sansarer kaaj*, Saraswati's sister would run all the errands for her, and help her with all her personal care tasks like bringing water for bathing, washing clothes, making the bed and helping her into the wheelchair. Manju's *dada* (elder brother) used to make her feel special by buying gifts only for her. 'During Puja, even if he never bought anything for the others, he would always give me a small gift. If there was any *ashanti* (lack of peace, referring to tensions, turmoil, strife) in the house, he always supported me. He used to take to me to school on his cycle especially if I had been ill or had fever.'

For Manju, being perceived as special and different meant that she was left out of the activities her brothers and sisters were involved in. 'My *dida* (maternal grandmother) was over protective and used to tell my brothers and sisters not to involve me in their games, as she was afraid I would get hurt. She would constantly scold them and say "don't do that to her" or "she can't do that".' While Manju's parents never tried to represent her as weak and incapable, they used to give her special privileges like giving in to her demands even while rejecting those of her siblings. 'I got whatever I wanted. My *sejda* (third brother, older to respondent) and *sejdi* (third sister, older to respondent) used to be the most jealous of my privileged position.' Creation of difference between the disabled girl and her siblings sometimes led to strained relations between the brothers and sisters, even in childhood and adolescence. Saraswati, who spent the first few years of her life living with her maternal grandparents and aunts because her mother was unable to care for her properly in the face of increased responsibilities at home and other small children, recalls that after moving back to live with her family, her *borobhai* (older of two younger brothers) was antagonistic towards her as he was jealous of the fact that she needed a lot of care from their mother. 'He was always rude and mean to her, not attending to any of her requests for help in daily tasks.'

Extended family members, like grandparents, paternal and maternal uncles and aunts, also contributed to this process of creation of difference. Chobi feels that her grandparents and uncles and aunts used to pamper her, not only because she was disabled but also because she was the only child in the family, as none of her *kaka*s had children. 'They listened to my every demand. *Dadu* (grandfather) was my friend and we would sit and chat, talk, play word games and laugh for hours together. *Dida* would take me outside the house and to the neighbouring houses, so that I could meet other children. If I wanted any doll or toy, I just had to tell my *kaka*s.' Asha's *kaka*s and *kakima*s always ensured that, despite not being able to walk, she always participated in the family activities. During festivals, especially Durga Puja, her *kaka*s ensured that she went with them to see the idols near their house. 'They would take me every year, sometimes in their arms, sometimes by cycle, and if I refused, they would say why should you stay back alone? If there was a *jatra* (play) being staged in the village, *ma* and *kakima*s would insist on taking me along with them. My *kakima* used to say, "Can't she have any aspirations?"'

Special privileges granted to the girls at home because of their impairments marked them out as distinct from their siblings in different ways. When Smita learnt to bathe all by herself, her *mama* was so happy that he immediately went and got a new bucket and mug for her from the bazaar. Whenever Smita and her family used to visit their paternal relatives who lived in their ancestral home in Midnapore, Smita would be cosseted by them and whatever she asked for was delivered. 'My *jethu* (father's elder brother) was my favourite, as whenever I made any demands, he would meet them immediately. Before going to the bazaar, Jethu would ask me especially "what do you want?" I would say whatever I wanted and he would bring it for me however expensive it was.'

In Bengal, most girls play with dolls and *khelna bati* (toy utensils), enacting the way their mothers manage their *sansar* and household work. Disabled girls also played with their sisters and female cousins, with the same toys, whether it was in rural households or in urban family settings. Agatha remembers that as she couldn't move around much, she used to play mostly 'sitting down' games with her brother and sister with dolls and *khelna bati*. Saraswati, being severely disabled, could not 'cook' but she would readily eat the 'meals prepared by her other cousins in her *mamabari* (maternal grandparent's house). Chobi, who is an only child, would play with the children next door, but as she was not able to use her hands much, 'they would cook and cut vegetables while I sat and watched'. Girls with mild and moderate disabilities played other more energetic games with their sisters and cousins, which needed physical exertion, like *lukochuri* (hide and seek) and catching the ball. In Asha's village when she was a small child, her friends always included her in games like *kabaddi*, as 'they felt I was lucky for them'. In the city, growing up with two brothers, Krishna was interested only in playing with marbles with her brothers and the neighbourhood boys on the terrace or in the backyard. 'I never played *kit-kit* (hopscotch), which usually all girls play. There was very little space to play, so most of the children would play games like hide and seek. I was not very interested, maybe because of my disability.'

Interactions with friends and other children also served to underscore the difference between the disabled girl and these other children. While Mita's friends expressed concern for her, the younger boys in their locality and in her school used to tease her. 'Maybe they wanted to show how strong they were and that I was weaker because of my polio affected leg. They called me *langda* (cripple), *pa khora* (lame legs), etc.' But Mita tried to ignore such comments as she felt that 'to protest against their hurtful words was to invite more and worse comments. I felt bad because these comments were really true as my leg is really like this'. Smita's siblings' friends refused to include her in their games because she was disabled. 'I used to feel sad and would think "why am I so different from the others? Why did they punish me like this?"' Aparna remembers that children in the village would tease her by calling her names like *khudi* (lame girl) or *lang lange* (having floppy feet).

The issue of sending the disabled girl to school becomes the basis for the creation of further differences, not by the family and neighbourhood but by the larger society as well. As these are girls with locomotor impairment, none of them would have any trouble in studying in 'mainstream' schools near to their homes. But the degree of impairment, construction of her disability, family and cultural ideologies and physical barriers, all influence the extent to which girls were able to access and profit from the educational systems available. Girls with mild to moderate impairments and living mainly in the city have been able to take advantage of the opportunities available, while girls with severe disabilities living in the villages either never went to school or dropped out after receiving some primary education. Although the primary school is just across their house, Saraswati's parents never thought of sending her to school, as she could 'neither move nor speak properly'. Saraswati's father feels that 'she didn't have the capability to study. How could we expect the school to admit her, when she could not even sit up properly? All her younger siblings went to school, but she couldn't because of her disability.' Saraswati is now convinced that her parents differentiated between her siblings and herself on account of her disability by denying her a chance to go to school.

Chobi never went to school, as there were no schools in the area that were ready to accept her as a student. Her parents tried at almost all the schools in the area and even approached a residential institution for mentally challenged children for admission. While the general schools refused to give her admission because they could not keep a girl in her condition in the classroom, the special school refused on the grounds that as she didn't have a mental disability they couldn't possibly accommodate her with the other students. Smita used to feel both angry and sad when she used to see her younger siblings go to school. Her mother had told her that the local corporation school refused to admit her because of her disability. Although she also wanted to go to school, she slowly accepted that while 'they (her siblings) could be admitted to any school, the same school wouldn't take me. Will a normal school admit a disabled student? At that time, it was unheard of.'

Mita got admission in school much later than other children because of the treatment she was undergoing to correct her impairment and because her mother felt that she would be able to cope up with her studies. Manju's father insisted on admitting her to a school near to their home as he was not in favour of sending her to a school further away from the house, because he felt that she wouldn't be able to manage the travel everyday. When Sulekha's grandfather first took her to the village school, she was denied admission. 'They were afraid that I would fall if the other children pushed me, or that I would not be able to come to school regularly. Even when *dadu* reassured them that he would ensure that I was regular in school and that nothing untoward would happen inside the class, they refused to admit me.' When the NGO supporting her produced a Government of India directive regarding admission of disabled children in mainstream school, the principal of the school reluctantly allowed her entry into the village school.

Agatha had been admitted to a nursery school run by nuns when she was around four years old. After two years of studying in that school, and being carried there and back by her mother, and by the nuns inside the school, Agatha got admission in a reputed primary school in Kolkata. However, at the time of admission, the school authorities had clearly told her mother that she would have the responsibility of taking her up the stairs to the classroom and then back down again. Agatha used to feel embarrassed when her mother would do so everyday as the other children would be smiling and pointing at her. But the most embarrassing moments were when the school authorities found that she had urine incontinence, and despite her being in nappies and plastic panties, decided to make her sit outside the classroom near the door so that the other children would not be bothered by the smell. Agatha recalls, 'The other children used to keep complaining "she smells, we cannot sit with her." I was so ashamed and mortified.' After three months of bearing such treatment, the school summoned her parents and told them to make her study from home and bring her to school only for the exams. Agatha's mother was so angry that she immediately took her out of the school. Agatha says that it was the most painful and embarrassing way to realize that she was different from all the other children.

Of all the girls, two from the villages and one from the city have never gone to school—Saraswati as her parents felt she wouldn't be able to learn, Aparna due to financial reasons and Chobi because schools refused to admit her; five completed primary schooling and could not continue—Jahanara, Asha and Sandhya because the high schools were far away and it was difficult for them to commute, Anita and Salema because they were not too good in studies; two—Rita and Sulekha have completed high school; three of the girls living in the city or near urban towns—Mita, Krishna and Manju have completed graduation; Agatha has completed her postgraduation while two girls living in the city have attended special schools. For girls with mild to moderate disabilities, parents stressed the need for education because they realized and accepted that their daughter had to be capable of supporting herself financially, as gender roles available to other women might be closed to her. Anita's mother felt that education was the only salvation for her daughter who wouldn't be able to 'work like a woman', and would help her to get a job, and earn a living. Rita recalls that from childhood her mother used to always stress the need for her studying and doing well, in spite of the problems she faced travelling to the school. Krishna's mother used to tell her that while her brothers would be able to indulge in hard labour, she would not be able to do so and hence she should study hard. The teachers in the schools were also of a similar opinion recalls Manju, who feels that they used to encourage her in her studies because they had implicitly accepted and wanted her to accept and understand that the lifestyle available to other girls would be closed for her.

> They would tell me that I could not afford to neglect my education, as some other girls may. They felt that my disability should compel me to study properly as the difference between me and the other girls was not just a physical difference of having a leg that didn't function as it should, but was something much more than that. It was like a goad for me pushing me to do well in studies. So they felt that I shouldn't behave like the other girls and should take my studies seriously. They would continuously tell me that I would have to stand on my feet and be self-sufficient.

Disabled girls are introduced gradually into the gendered socio-cultural ideologies about able-bodied girls within families, in the neighbourhood and at school, and learn to recognize their difference from their sisters and girls of their age. Although the experience is mainly of positive discrimination, where she is treated with utmost care and is cosseted by the entire family, this creates differences between the girl and her siblings, which has implication for their relationship over their growing up years and also in adulthood. The exemption of disabled girls from household work or assigning work that is considered to be 'light' or relatively easy to perform serves to highlight differences with other siblings and reinforces ableist ideologies that decree disabled people as unfit to participate in familial and social processes. On the other hand, families sometimes took extra care to ensure that the disabled girl was not left out of family and social functions and underscored the fact that she was allowed to have desires and aspirations like other women. The girls experienced the processes of gender socialization like other girls in the family, as this was the primary basis of their identities, while their impairment was something which interfered with such socialization in a variety of ways. The social milieu outside the home was however, not as kind to these girls, who had painful encounters in the public domain as well as in schools. While parents and teachers emphasized that these girls needed an education more than other girls, the process of differentiated entailed encounters with the outside world, which reveals the gendered/ableist ideologies harboured not just by individuals but also by educational institutions.

Living the Difference

Disabled girls come to realize and accept that they are different from their non-disabled sisters, and that they cannot aspire to achieve what is subsumed in the ideological construct of the '*bhalo meye*' (good girl/woman), implying a girl with functionally perfect body. A *bhalo meye* symbolizes a girl, with a unimpaired body and capabilities, one who is seen as potentially capable of taking on increasing amount of responsibility to cater to the needs of her natal and affinal families, one whose productive and reproductive capacities blossom and develop from adolescence to adulthood. Disabled girls become aware of their difference in gait and ability during adolescence and experience a sense of failure at not being a '*bhalo meye*'. For severely disabled girls, the process of living the difference begins in early childhood. Agatha used to see children running around and would ask her mother why she also couldn't do so. '*Ma* used to tell me that God has made you very different and you have other things to do in life, so you don't have to run around like the others. Somehow I realized that there was something wrong with me but what it was I didn't fully comprehend then, but sometimes used to feel sad that I couldn't run, skip and play like the other children.' Sandhya had accepted her difference from her sisters and the resultant curtailment of activities. But at adolescence she started feeling embarrassed whenever she went out in public as she was ashamed of the way in which she moved.

Girls realize the nature of their difference from their other siblings, especially their sisters and female cousins, in late childhood or early adolescence more sharply than they did in their early years. They recall that in childhood, there was greater equality among them because they all were unaware of the social construction of disability and disabled people, and hence developed a relationship of deep affection, of sharing of daily activities like bathing, eating and playing. Girls felt more comfortable and less self-conscious about moving by crawling or limping, as they had not yet internalized social perceptions that deem crawling as degrading. Thus, going out of the house crawling, to the playground with siblings, friends and cousins was not so uncommon especially in the rural areas. Asha remembers that whenever her sisters used to go out to play, they insisted that she go along with them. 'As we were close in age and I was quite thin, my second sister would hitch me on her hip and carry me sometimes, if we were going a distance from our home. I never felt embarrassed at that time.' Sulekha's friends and sisters would play in the evening in the big field beside her house. As Sulekha couldn't run around, she would sit there and watch them play in the evenings after school. Similarly, Sandhya used to go to watch her siblings play in the big field in their village. 'As I could not play with them, I would slowly crawl and later used my crutches to go and sit in the courtyard of the nearby mandir. I would watch them, and sometimes when they would play catch, and I would do too but on my knees.'

As the disabled girl and her non-disabled sisters realize she is different, they deal with it in different ways. Feelings of jealousy about her non-disabled 'unflawed' sister prompted Saraswati, who shared all her sister's personal toiletries, to refuse to allow her to use any of her own clothes or other trinkets.

I had this competition with her because she was 'normal' and my parents relied a lot on her. When I got my own room, I never allowed her to sleep in my room. She would come and help me with all my personal tasks like cleaning the room, washing my clothes, etc., but why should I give her my space? She could go wherever she wanted by herself, I couldn't.

Smita, on the other hand, had to face her sister's jealousy, because of the special attention she got from her family members. Her sister never told any of her friends about Smita, and neither did she ever acknowledge her presence when her friends came to visit. 'She was ashamed of me. When her friends came home and saw me, they also ignored me and it was then that I realized that my sister couldn't accept my disability.'

Training in household work usually begins for all girls in late childhood with mothers assigning different tasks like fetching water, washing utensils, peeling vegetables, cleaning the rooms, etc., that are aimed at preparing them for their adult roles of wife and mother. From the time a girl in the rural areas is 6–7 years old, she starts helping out with the work at home. The girls with the most severe disabilities, especially those with cerebral palsy that affects both their hands and legs, are the only ones who are left out of this kind of gendered training. Girls with mild to moderate disabilities found themselves being assigned household work, although the imperative of taking up the responsibility varies from family to family. All girls, disabled or not, were expected to take up some part of the household work, but differences were created between sisters with regard to the kind of work assigned to them, with only the lighter or easier tasks assigned to them, especially if there were elder sisters/sisters-in-law in the family.

Manju remembers that although her elder sisters had to help with kitchen work, she was always assigned duties like making the bed and arranging the clothes on the *alna* (wooden rack on which clean clothes are kept after washing). She was never allowed to do any cooking, as '*ma* used to say your leg is bad, if there is an accident then you will be burnt. So I wasn't allowed to work on the coal or wood oven or even the stove. I would cut and wash the vegetables for cooking.' Jahanara's mother never had to ask her to do much work at home, not only because of her disability but also because she had many sisters who were there to step in.

> Once or twice when I tried to take the utensils to the *ghat* (paved or log carved steps leading to the pond) of the pond for washing, I lost balance and fell badly. So I was not allowed to do all that. Sometimes *ammi* (mother) would allow me to help with the kitchen work which meant making *rotis*, cutting the small pieces of wood into smaller bits for using as fuel and to put the kerosene in the lanterns.

Smita, who was the eldest among the siblings rarely helped her mother with the work. 'Even if *ma* sometimes asked me to do small things like shelling peas, my sister or brothers would say why should didi (elder sister) do it? We'll do it.'

For disabled girls, the ability to engage in and complete the household chores was one way of lessening the difference that was constructed between her and her other siblings. Mita related that she laboured to do all the work her sisters were assigned, even though her mother would forbid her to do so.

When my sisters used to go to fill drinking water from the communal tap, I used to tag along with them, and would carry the bucket back home. Sometimes I fell and the water spilt also but I just wanted to do all that they did. Ma used to say '*tui parbi na*' (you can't) so I wanted to show her I could.

Asha, who did some of the household work like cutting vegetables for cooking and sweeping the house, recalls that whenever she asked to do any work, her mother would say, 'you don't have to do it or it will be tiring for you. But the only difference between my sisters and me was that they could walk and so they do things like bringing water from the pond or carrying things.' Asha's mother explained that she didn't feel like giving any work to Asha as she was disabled and she wouldn't be able to manage.

I never let her do anything much as I used to feel she would have difficulties. She crawls using her hands, so how can she carry anything? How can I ask her to help with the household work? I asked my other daughters to help with tasks like cutting the vegetables or bringing the water as I knew once my daughters got married, they would be forced to do all this work in their *sasur bari*.

For Asha, the message that she was not 'perfect' or 'normal', and hence didn't need training for responsibilities after marriage, was evident from her mother's exhortations to her sisters to learn household work properly, as they would have to do it when they got married. 'I never had to hear any comment like that as they had accepted from when I was young that I would not be getting married.'

As they grew up and widened their spheres of interaction, disabled girls increasingly came to realize their difference from other people and the ramifications of their impairments, which also fuelled different feelings of anger, bitterness and deep resentment. Anita's neighbours used to call her with different nicknames, which although sounding affectionate, were actually derogatory like *Kochi* (young one, also meaning the naïve), *Tepu* (snot nosed one), *Nono* (the smallest one). 'No one ever bothered to use the name given by my parents. This made me very angry as people joked about my height or laughed at me. But I never gave it much importance as, if I showed them that it bothered me then they would step up the teasing. They are like barking dogs, should I bark back at them?' Other children and people on roads stared, pointed towards and teased the girls because they were crawling or walking with a very different gait. It is this very difference that was given the form of devaluation and made the girls an object of ridicule. Girls recall that boys were more derisive of them and their impairments. In Mita's neighbourhood, boys would loudly call her '*shalik pakhir thang khora* (see the brown sparrow limping)'. Manju was labelled as *langda* or *khudi* (lame girl/women) as 'I would stand out like a sore thumb at that time when very few people had heard about or seen disabled people. Everyone would stare at me like I was a novelty. I think the boys teased me more as they wanted to prove that I was lesser than them.'

The first contact with the outside world began at school, with the girls not only meeting their teachers, but also other students in their class. Access to primary education, whether in rural or in urban set ups, has become evident with the implementation of the programme for Sarva Shiksha Abhiyaan. As most of the primary schools are located in the village itself, parents living in rural areas are also encouraged to send all their children to school, though girls get assigned household work as they grow older. While differences between boys and girls exist with regard to access to education, the divide begins primarily at the level of secondary education. In case of the disabled girls, the scenario is the same, although the reasons for their dropping out were both gender and impairment related. However, access to education is also influenced by financial condition of the family, rural or urban locales and attitude of the parents. While the physical access to schools and the financial implications become the determining factors in accessing higher education, parent's and family members' ideas regarding the future of the disabled girl and her difference from other girls, determine the continuing of education.

The comprehension of difference gets crystallized here in face of not only different physical and material realities but also from the way in which a non-disabled strange world looked at and treated them. Sandhya, whose school was a 10–15 minutes walk from her house for '*bhalo*' (good meaning non-disabled) children, says that she had to leave 30 minutes before school started, as she used to crawl all the way to school. With callipers and crutches, Sulekha used to take much longer to walk to school than her sisters. Sisters and friends helped out by carrying their school bags, which is difficult to carry while one is crawling or trying to manoeuvre rough paths on callipers. In the rainy season, when the roads became difficult to traverse for all people, Asha, who used to crawl to school, recalls that she would reach school 'dirty and completely muddied. It was so embarassing'. The road to Mita's school was *kaccha* (unpaved) and she used to face a lot of problems in walking to school in the rainy season. 'I used to reach school totally drenched in slush. My siblings were able to hang onto paddy plants and walk through the slushy mud. But my heavy callipers resulted in my falling down many times.'

It is in schools that disabled girls started realizing the differences between them and the other children, both through the interaction with the children and from the messages they received from their teachers. As they started growing older, girls also came to realize their differences in the subtle ways of different practices, necessitated by the nature of their disability. Jahanara envied the other children who would wear boots to school, as she could only ever wear slippers because of her weak leg. She used to feel bad about it but knew that she would have to manage with slippers because she was disabled.

Jahanara relates that she resented being restrained from playing games along with the other girls in school. 'The teacher used to ask me to watch while the others played, and the only time I was allowed to participate was when there were free hand exercises in the P.T. period. I also wanted to try the ring toss or the skipping rope. I wished I was like the other girls and could do all that.'

In the villages, girls drop out of secondary school, mainly because the high schools are in faraway villages. For disabled girls it becomes nearly impossible to traverse such distances considering their mode of mobility. Asha, who wanted to study further, was forced to drop out of school, as the high school was nearly 4 km. away from her home. There were very few means of transport available and from the family no one could be spared to make the journey for her twice in a day. 'As I can only go by crawling, it became extremely difficult to go to school. My father did not have the time to take me as he would then have to miss work.' Asha's mother explained that, even for a *bhalomanush* (good person meaning simple, helpful, non-disabled) it was a big hassle, and for Asha it would have been a nightmare to even attempt to continue her education. Financial reasons forced Sandhya to discontinue her studies, while Jahanara was forced to drop out of high school by her father as he was afraid that the political violence in the area would affect his school-going daughter adversely. He was scared that his daughters would catch the attention of the local *goondas* (thugs) and their and his honour would be compromised.

For girls with mild to moderate disabilities living in urban or suburban settings, continuing with education is relatively less difficult, and they receive a lot of encouragement from their family as well as their teachers. Krishna remembers that her mother was always very particular about her studies and made it clear that she would have to struggle more in life compared to her brothers and other girls because she was disabled. Krishna had to walk 2 km. to school every day with all the other students, despite having problems in walking long distances with her callipers. 'Going to school every day was a big struggle as I would get sores on my legs and feet where the callipers brushed against the skin. In the rainy season, as those roads get waterlogged very easily, I had to wade through knee or hip-deep water to get to school.' Mita, who was always sickly, struggled a lot in her pursuit of a degree and though she passed the examinations, her results were 'poor' and this affected her chances of further education. Rita shifted to a residential institution in Kolkata for completing her education, as she knew that she would not be able to continue attending school while living in the village, as the high school was nearly 5 km. away.

The material reality of the body, the impairments, is thus impossible to deny or overcome, and as they grow up the girls learn to struggle against, accept and manage their bodies according to gendered constructions as far as possible. Anita, who is of very short stature, was aware of the stares of people whenever she went out of the neighbourhood. 'I used to feel ashamed of my height and myself. I used to feel that I should be ashamed of being short, and accept that whenever I went out people would make fun of me. If and when I went out, I would walk behind my *boudis* (elder sisters-in-law) covered with the *anchal* (shoulder pleats) of their sarees, so that no one could see me).' Sometimes people stop her on the road and laugh at and tease her, calling her a *bamun* (dwarf) or joker.

Disabled girls find themselves marked out and looked upon as something different, focusing mainly on their disability. The general reaction is of benevolent curiosity, kindness and concern, although some responses are of disdain, pity and revulsion. Aparna feels that most people show *daya* (kindness) and *karuna* (pity) towards her when she is in the market or in public transport. Sulekha remembers that if she fell down, most people would help her up, but very few laughed at her plight. In the city, however, Chobi recalls that when her mother used to take her shopping with her, some people were rude enough to comment loudly about how different she was from other children. 'Sometimes in the shops people would stare at me as they hadn't seen any one like that before, but they didn't say anything. People would ask questions like how did this happen? How do you manage with her? What can she do?'

Girls are pampered, cosseted, protected and cared for within the family, creating differences between them and their brothers and sisters, sometimes in subtle ways and at others in an overt manner. While all this reinforces the images of the disabled as weak and dependent and leads to differential treatment of siblings within the family, it also results in over-protection of the disabled girl in different household and familial practices. Some of the girls felt restricted by such ideologies and practices and believe that their parents could have challenged them with coping with their daily lives in a better manner rather than devaluing them with assumptions of incapability. The sense of security provided within the family made the harsher interactions with the outside world more painful and difficult to accept and reconcile for the disabled girl. After having enjoyed a privileged status within the family, neighbourhood and public spaces as well as schools were experienced as oppressive and degrading, where one was judged solely by the prescribed standards of idealized normality and not by the realities of their capacities and capabilities. Though ideologies negate the capacities of the disabled girls, their lived realities often differ as they experience, negotiate and tailor the needs of their impaired bodies to the performance of the feminine self.

Note

1. Special day allocated for worshipping *Saraswati*, the Hindu goddess of learning.

CHAPTER V

Embodiment
Struggling to be a *Bhalo Meye*

My disability is my identifying mark. No one thinks of me as a woman.

The body is understood as socially constructed, interpreted and experienced and becomes a physical site from and through which a person knows and interacts with the social world. It is constantly and systematically produced, sustained and presented in everyday life, realized and actualized through a variety of socially regulated practices or activities that are needed to sustain social order at the micro-level. The possession of a body with specific features becomes crucial for everyday recognition and identification of persons within any society as well as for interpreting individuals' interactions with their bodies and through their bodies with the world around them (Turner 1996; Davis 1997). Thus, embodiment can be understood as the process whereby the materiality of the body is interpreted through the gendered/ableist cultural constructions that situate the female/impaired body in space, time and culture. Socio-cultural constructions of the ideal or 'normal' female body are internalized through processes of socialization and influence the thoughts and experiences of disabled women in their daily lives. In this chapter, such processes are unravelled through an exploration of the ways in which women with disabilities react to, redefine and come to resolve their gendered notions with the needs of their bodies and the socio-cultural and physical environment in which they are located. The chapter further illuminates the ways in which notions of femininity, sexuality and marriageability are used by disabled women to redefine and negotiate the performance of their impaired bodies in their daily lives to achieve a gendered life. The last section of the chapters explores the interactions of gendered/impaired bodies with the public domain and reveals the agency employed by disabled women in engaging with and negotiating public spaces.

* Certain sections of this chapter have been published in *Economic and Political Weekly*, vol. XLV, no.17, April 2010 and as part of a chapter in an edited volume entitled *Disability Studies in India*, ed. Renu Adlakha, New Delhi, 2013.

Adolescent/Adulthood Experiences: Reconciling Gender and Disability

The girls internalize and are guided from a young age by social attitudes, expectations and modes of behaviour considered appropriate for women. As they grow up, they learn and internalize the ideal of a *bhalo meye* in all senses of the term. This idealized concept, which is closely connected to the notions of the female body and what is expected from it, from physical beauty, functional capacities, productive and reproductive connotations, which govern the daily lives of all women. Bengali gender culture upholds ideal of the body, physical appearance and functionality that is considered to be desirable in all women, especially if they are to fulfil the role of wife and mother. The concept of *bhalo meye* is used by disabled girls in a dual sense, referring to women with unimpaired 'normal' bodies as well as to women who conform to and actualize the ideal notions that the gender culture attributes to women. Young girls internalize an image of the ideal body and the particular kind of physical beauty, notions of appropriate and acceptable feminine comportment as well as functional capacities that is desirable among women. This ideal, however, varies from prescribing acceptable range of height, weight, skin tone, arrangement of features and behaviour patterns that determine one's dress, appearance, hairstyle, etc., which are learnt from the verbal and visual messages projected by other women and the media. Disabled girls, also socialized into such body ideals, however, find it difficult to accommodate the imperatives of their impaired bodies to some of these notions and prescribed behaviour patterns which become increasingly important to all girls as they grow up.

As children, disabled girls are pampered and cosseted, and differences created within the home between siblings, liberally exempting the girl from dealing with personal and household work in order to accommodate her impairment. However, as they grow into adolescence and increasingly internalize the notions of ideal womanhood, they come to realize their difference from their sisters, especially in terms of their impairment and its effect on their movements, personal care and household chores. In their daily lives, women grow up negotiating their impaired bodies and the routine performance of these activities within the household. The thrust on achieving the status of a *bhalo meye* makes it imperative for both girls and their families to strive for being able to be independent and to be and act like a woman.

'Hata Chala' *(walking and moving around)*: *First step to self-dependence*

As documented in the previous chapter, one of the first reactions of parents was to seek a cure for their daughter with an impairment, so that she would be able to walk, be able to take care of herself and be as 'normal' as the other girls in the family. Of all the girls, only three of them have never attempted to seek medical treatment—for Chobi the severity of her impairment and its slow progression precluded such a quest while for Anita and Salema the mild nature of their impairments did not necessitate such an intervention. For all of the other girls, their parents wanted them to become as independent as her impairment would allow, not only for participating in daily life activities, but also to reduce the visible impact of the disability, so that her future chances in life, especially of marriage would not be affected. Girls underwent surgery, physiotherapy and fitting with mobility aids so that they could walk better, straighter and like other 'normal' people.

At present ten of them use some kind of mobility aid, ranging from wheelchairs and tri-wheelers for the severely disabled to callipers and crutches. Of the others, two more had received callipers and crutches but discontinued its use within a few months; this was mainly because the mobility aids were not suited to the rough and uneven beaten tracks in the villages; also because they used to leave home only occasionally, either for school or very rarely to relatives outside the village. Mobility aids were experienced as painful and restrictive and girls, who could not use their callipers at home for daily life activities like bathing and toileting or even household work, discontinued its use. At home or in familiar spaces, where acceptance is assumed and presentation of the feminine self is not so imperative, girls prefer not to use their mobility aids as it hampers their performance of household work or attending to their daily needs. Asha recalls that within the home and with family it didn't matter how she moved around, as everyone knew of her disability. Within the home, Sulekha moves on her hands and feet as she can do things faster and move around with more ease than with her calliper. On the other hand, Manju stressed that she always felt more comfortable in her callipers as she realized that she could walk straight when wearing it. Without the callipers she has to walk with a hand to her knee, but that emphasized her impairment and attracted attention in public spaces. The mobility aid helped Manju to present a more 'normal' image of herself. 'Without my callipers I would have had to use crutches all my life or walk with a terribly lopsided gait.'

The use of mobility aids is attuned to not only the needs of their disability but also to the notions of femininity internalized through the processes of socialization. Sandhya and Asha both felt that the metallic aid attached to leather boots diminished their sense of themselves as women. Mita recalls that 'the calliper was very visible especially because I used to wear skirts at that age. Somewhere it clashed with my idea of a feminine self.' She hated them. Sulekha feels more dignified in public places while walking in callipers rather than crawling around. She feels it enables her to project herself as a 'normal' woman. With newer technology coming in, Sulekha requested the technicians to adapt her mobility aid to feminine codes of dress and notions of beauty so that it now allows her to give full expression to her feminine tastes, rather than the older heavy boots accentuating her impairment. 'I am happy that I can wear my calliper inside my salwar when I go out such that the calliper is not visible to all. I bought new fashionable chappals to go with the new callipers. Now I can wear platform heels also if I want with my calliper.'

The social valuation of perfect bodies not only accentuates visible differences but when coupled with teasing comments and taunts, gives rise to feelings of inferiority and devaluation. Girls, who are unable to walk, feel a sense of shame because of the way in which they move, either by crawling or by dragging their hips, which makes them the object of ridicule and pity in public. These feelings get crystallized during adolescence, and are manifested in diverse ways of dealing with the shame, one of which is to lead a reclusive existence. Asha started feeling ashamed of herself and the way in which she moved after she came back from the rehabilitation centre during her early teenage years. 'Everyone around me would be walking and I would be crawling along. I was ashamed of going out like this, as people would stare at me all the time. So I stopped going out of the house.' Sandhya used to feel ashamed that her elderly father had to carry her to different places before she got her tricycle. 'It was so embarrassing and mortifying to be carried by my father. When I insisted on moving by myself, I slipped and fell so many times that he had to carry me again.'

Chobi started feeling ashamed of being carried to different places, especially in public spaces and going out thus became a source of continuous shame and a reinforcement of her incapability. When she was younger, her *baba* and *kakas* would carry her to all social and religious programmes or hire a rickshaw to take her to the different Durga Puja[1] pandals[2] in the locality. But once she grew older and became heavy, these visits stopped overtly because of the upheaval involved in carrying her down four flights of stairs to go outside, and carrying her into and out of the pandals. But Chobi confessed that she herself used to refuse to go out as in the puja pandal she used to feel as if she were an object of amusement or scorn caught in the pitiful stares of people. 'I used to feel like an animal in a zoo. Everyone would stare at me, as if I was someone from another world, an extraordinary thing, something people had never seen before.'

The performance of a feminine self becomes central as they grow up, especially in public spaces where they encounter the 'gaze' more than in familiar surroundings. Girls seek to minimize the visual impact of their physical impairment by adopting gaits that seem 'normal' in order to gain greater acceptance. Although Sandhya moves by crawling within the home, she uses a tri-wheeler when she goes out. 'People realize I am disabled but they can never make out the extent of my disability when I drive my tri-wheeler down the road. To them, I am a woman, dressed well and that is the image I like to project. It is only when I start crawling that the admiring looks turn to one of pity.' Jahanara has taught herself to walk slowly and wear sarees, which conceal her disability effectively.

Amio to Meye *(I, too, am a girl): Dress and Accessories*

Ideologies about feminine modesty internalized are adapted to the needs of the girls and is reflected in the ways in which these women adhere to feminine modes of dressing or modify such notions to present themselves as women. Wanting to be identified and accepted as women, they wear 'feminine' clothes and adhering to feminine norms of beauty sometimes becomes imperative in order to prove their equality with other women. Women with mild to moderate disabilities adhere to acceptable feminine modes of dressing, as it is one way of asserting their femininity. However, in a certain way, as their sexuality is negated or denied, disabled girls sometimes find themselves frozen in adolescence in terms of dressing codes. Although popular attire for growing girls is the salwar kameez, the degree of disability determines the choice of clothes to a great extent and girls, who had been wearing skirts and blouses, continue to do so, citing convenience of movement in such clothes.

Asha says that she prefers to wear skirt-blouses or a nightgown, as they are easy to manage while crawling. '*Ma* cuts them short for me, so that I am well covered and yet when I crawl, the dress doesn't get very dirty nor is there too much cloth to encumber my movements.' Hence notions of modesty are tailored to the needs of their impaired bodies and different gaits. Girls who crawl prefer blouses and skirts, which can be hitched up and notched carefully at the thighs so that modesty is preserved and yet movement is easy. The adherence to adolescent dress codes is suggestive of arrested womanhood, and a slightly different code of modesty that allows them to wear such clothes for convenience. When Saraswati was younger, she used to wear pants and shirts as it was easier to put on and it helped her to move easily. But since she reached adolescence, she has been wearing only salwar kameezes or long frocks, skirts and blouses, which are usually gifts or bought for her by others. 'I would prefer to wear pants and shirts as it makes my crawling around easier. Salwar kameezes are helpful as they don't expose my legs to the people around.' Sandhya prefers to wear skirts and blouses rather than nightgowns and salwar kameezes, which restrict her movements and tear easily because of the way in which she moves. She finds going to the field for her toilet most embarrassing as despite trying to be modest, she is unable to adhere to the strict codes of feminine behaviour. 'Going to the toilet, I hitch up my clothes to knee level. Sometimes it is embarrassing in front of strangers or lots of people but what to do? People may stare and laugh but as a girl, I have my modesty and I try to preserve it as best as I can.'

Notions of feminine beauty drive some of the women to opt for makeup and jewellery. In a way it is an affirmation, to herself and people around of her femininity. Chobi remembers that she would ask her *ma* and *dida* to make her beautiful by applying lipstick. 'I like wearing *bindis* (mark worn between the eyebrows) and earrings, and got my ears pierced. Sometimes when I feel very dressy, I wear necklaces also. I wear long gowns at home in summer and salwar kameezes in winter. I like wearing such feminine attire like frocks and gowns.' Krishna says that she likes to think of herself as a woman based on 'my looks, my body, and myself. I wear jeans but even in my jeans I like to look as a woman'. Agatha elaborated, 'I want to be identified as a woman. I like to wear womanly clothes and I want to be known as a woman rather than anything else.' Other markers of a feminine self like having long hair, wearing jewellery and using makeup are accepted and employed to 'look like a woman' and thus be accepted as one. 'Now that I have grown my hair and am wearing long earrings and *bindis*, suddenly everyone has realized that I am a girl. My friends tell me that now I am looking like a girl and give me advice on make-up. I like the fact that my colleagues now identify me as a girl.'

Women are socialized into accepting the saree as the most suitable garb for them. However, very few of these women, and then too only the ones with mild disability, wear sarees on a regular basis. Agatha rarely wears sarees as she finds it difficult to manage one with her callipers and crutches. 'Someone has to help me wear a saree as I cannot do it myself, standing with my crutches. So I have given up on sarees now. During college days, I wore sarees for the farewell and welcome parties, as everyone else was also wearing and I wanted to be like them.' Asha, who wears skirts, would like to wear sarees but accepts that they would get dirty while crawling. 'It is very difficult to crawl around in a saree, especially outside the house as so much of cloth hampers one's movements.' Sandhya expresses her frustrations at not being able to wear a saree, when she states, 'How can I wear a saree? How can I possibly move about in a saree?'

Mita, who wears sarees regularly to work and whenever she goes out, feels comfortable in one as it makes her feel 'feminine'. 'I love to wear sarees, which I always wear outside the house. For me, it is a very feminine way of dressing.' However, there are drawbacks of wearing a saree. 'When I wear my calliper, the fold of the saree often gets stuck in the calliper and makes me lose balance.' Manju started wearing sarees regularly when she started working as she feels that the management in her office expected it of her, although no one forced her into it. For her, wearing the saree everyday became the symbol of reaffirmation of herself as a woman, and as it covered her calliper, very few people could discern that she was disabled. Now she wears sarees all the time, mostly because after marriage very few women wear salwar kameez. 'If I wear salwars, people will say "*beshi* (excessive) style".'

Some of the girls downplay their femininity by dressing conservatively, so as not to call any more attention to themselves that they already are subjected to, because of their impairments. Asha scorns at dressing in fine clothes and putting on make-up, and states that she never liked doing so from her childhood. 'It is not because I am like this—disabled. I don't like showing off to the world. I like dressing simply with just earrings and may be a bindi. Sometimes when I put on many things and look in the mirror I feel that I am too dressed up. Dressing up is not for me.' Sandhya reiterated the same sentiment when she asserted that she doesn't like *sajgoj* (dressing up). In the period that we were talking to each other, the marriage of her only niece was being fixed. When asked about whether she would dress up for her niece's marriage, she replied, 'Dress up at my niece's marriage? What will people say? Girls like us have no right to dress up.'

Gharer kaaj (*housework*)

The division of labour in Bengali families reflects the ideologies regarding roles of men and women in the family, with majority of the household tasks being performed by the women, while men are considered to be the breadwinners of the family. The training in household work begins early for daughters, with helping mothers with the different chores at home to taking care of younger siblings and finally to managing the home as preparation for her future role of wife and mother. However, such training presupposes that girls have reached a certain stage of independence in their personal care in order to start taking responsibility within the family. Ideologies regarding abilities of disabled girls and the actuality of their impairments deem that these girls are represented as dependent and incapable of dealing with increased responsibilities. For girls who are unable to manage or manage with difficulty their daily care, proving their independence in personal care becomes important to being recognized as a contributing member of the family.

In the villages, this process is further complicated by the physical environment, where ponds, which provide water for all personal and household tasks, are at a distance from the house. Asha learnt to independently bathe herself in the pond near her house, carrying her clothes over her shoulder and dragging the soap case along the ground. In Sandhya's village, the ponds being very far (nearly 500 m. away), her parents carried water to the courtyard of their home where she bathed. The pond where Rita bathes is very deep and has a steep descent to the water level. The only steps there are made of single bamboos with just one bamboo on the side for her support. Rita, because of her weak legs and shaky gait, has slipped and tumbled from the top into the mud at the lower level many times and hurt herself badly.

Household work mainly includes cooking, cleaning utensils, washing clothes, sweeping and swabbing the rooms, taking care of young children and elderly people. In rural areas, there are additional tasks like fetching drinking water, collecting firewood and tending to animals. Girls are trained by mothers and other women in the family from their teenage years to share, initially the easier and lighter tasks, and slowly as they grow older, cooking, cleaning and caring for younger siblings. Disabled girls, however, experience this process differently depending not only on their bodily deficits, but also on the milieu in which they are located and individual familial ideologies regarding the capacities of women with disabilities. Disabled women are considered incapable of engaging in most of these tasks because of their impairments, and both parents and the girls themselves feel that it was their impairment that was the basis of such creation of difference between them and their sisters. In adolescence, disabled girls were seldom asked to help with the household chores while their younger sisters were carefully coached. Mothers are afraid to assign tasks to their disabled daughters that involved moving around or carrying heavy loads. Asha's mother asks, 'Can she ever work like any of my other daughters?'

Families stress the ideological difference between *gharer kaaj* (house work) and *sansarer kaaj* (household work), and make it clear that while a disabled girl is assigned *gharer kaaj*, she is deemed unfit for *sansarer kaaj*, which includes taking care of the entire family and is seen as a task which is impossible for these women. While the *ghar* signifies only the home, *sansar* is conceptualized as the entire family and household, with social and cultural importance and entailing an entirely different set of responsibilities. Disabled women, assumed to be less capable and treated at par with children, are seen as incapable of shouldering the *sansarer kaaj*, though she may be capable of dealing with some of the work within the home. Thus, the nature of responsibilities assigned varies depending on the composition of the household and the degree of disability, although families have a tendency to treat the disabled daughter differently in terms of sharing the load of household work. At home, Sandhya's main responsibilities included cutting the vegetables and cooking, while her younger sister used to bring the water for drinking and cooking, and take the clothes and utensils to the *pukur ghat* (steps leading to pond, small tank of fresh water) for washing. Sandhya used to make puffed rice with her mother, dusting the rice and frying it to be consumed by the family. At that time, she also used to assist in the processing of the paddy once it was harvested from their fields and was in charge of spreading it out and drying it in the fields. Sandhya clarified that, 'I can do anything that can be done sitting down as I don't have any problems with my hands.'

Although disabled girls were treated differently from their sisters with regard to household work during adolescence, when the family faces a crisis situation or falls into difficult circumstances, disabled girls have to take more responsibility than they had been assigned till then. Mita's father's business started floundering when she was around ten years old, and all the members of their family had to start working. Her elder sisters dropped out of school and worked at a *khadi* (handspun and handwoven cloth) factory nearby, her mother started stitching clothes for a local tailor and her brothers worked in their father's shop. Mita, as a disabled girl, was not considered fit to take up any kind of work. As she remained at home, she took over from her mother and elder sisters the major responsibility of cooking from her mother and elder sisters. 'They (the family) sympathized with my condition and always thought that I was needy and weak, that I would not be able to cope up or manage.' Mita learnt all the household work at this age, from cooking, cleaning, washing to putting mud on walls, tending to their cow, cutting, hay, etc. 'Cooking was my primary responsibility, which also meant having to light the coal oven and wood stoves. My sisters would bring the water for cooking and drinking before they left for work, but all the rest of the work, I managed on my own.'

In families where the disabled daughter is the only girl other than the mother, the responsibility for household work falls on her shoulders in her mother's absence. When Krishna's mother was hospitalized for a prolonged period, she had to step into her mother's shoes, managing the cooking, directing the servants as well as caring for her sick mother. 'I was forced to take up all the responsibility for the home then, from cooking to cleaning washing and supervising the work of the maid at home.' Krishna, who was in high school at the time, feels that she suddenly had to become an adult and care for the men of the family as well as her mother. At that time she felt scared and lost but now feels that the experience helped her to assume the role of a woman, despite her impairments.

Life in the village is generally more difficult than that in the city, as women are expected to engage in different tasks that require physical strength and stamina like fetching water from the well, carrying clothes and utensils to the pond for washing and back, tending to large animals like cows and working in the fields. One of the most important tasks is fetching drinking water from wells or taps which may be located at a distance from their home, and inability to do that is perceived as incapability to manage the household. While the girls and their families acknowledge that bringing water from the well is difficult and they need help with it, washing clothes and cleaning utensils fall within the regular responsibilities of disabled women. Sulekha washes the clothes of the entire family at the ghat of their pond, though she needs help from her sister or mother to carry the bucket full of clothes to and from the pond and also to put the clothes out for drying.

Yet families tend to undermine the capabilities of the girls and negate their efforts towards the household work, stressing the fact that they are unable to do all the work independently and that they always need help. Sulekha's mother and sister loudly proclaim, 'how will she work, she cannot walk', even though she had been managing the entire household and cooking for her father and brother when her mother used to visit her natal home. From the time she was 14 years old, Sulekha has also been cleaning utensils and washing clothes for the entire family, needing help only to carry the utensils and clothes back and forth from the pond. Sandhya's elder sister pointed out that she was dependent on others while performing household tasks. 'Sandhya can make rice by boiling the *dhan* (paddy), but she needs someone to put the heavy pans on the wood oven and to remove it again when it is done. She can sit and stir the pot but can't pour, and needs someone to help her.'

Cooking is one responsibility traditionally associated with women. For disabled women, who aspire to be recognized as women, cooking becomes a marker for claiming equal status with other women. Although their mothers are still in charge of the kitchen, disabled girls have learnt how to cook, even if it is to fill the gap when their mothers are not at home. Asha's mother doesn't allow any of her daughters to cook on a regular basis but when she goes to visit her married daughters, it is Asha who cooks for her father and brother. However, she admits that she has to depend on her brother to fetch the water and help her washing the utensils. Sulekha, who also cooks for the entire family whenever her mother is away, feels that she is not capable of managing the task alone. With parents growing older and sisters moving away after marriage, disabled women have to lend their support to their mothers at home. Agatha recalls that when she was growing up, her only responsibility towards home was to cut the salad and lay the table for the entire family. Now, as the only child left with her parents, she helps her mother cook lunch especially on holidays and weekends, in addition to laying the table. When their maid doesn't come, she helps with the washing of utensils and cleaning of the kitchen after cooking.

Paid Work: Ideologies and Practice

The ideology around work in Bengal has always considered women's income as secondary to that of the men in the family. The ideologies regarding work have been influenced by middle and babu class ideas, who sought to confine their women within the walls of the home as a symbol of prestige and power. However, women from middle and upper middle class families living in the urban areas have increasingly been seeking work outside the home, not just for economic reasons but also for independence and utilizing their education. In the villages and poorer families, although women have always worked for a living to support the family, their contributions are either subsumed within family finances or dismissed as supportive to the income of the men in the family. For disabled women in such cultural contexts, sometimes earning a living is imperative in order to survive, but many look for work in order to keep themselves engaged and prove their worth to the family and community around.

Ideologies of work posit disabled girls as incapable of handling income generating work outside the home because of the travel and physical stress involved. Among the eighteen women, at the time of the study, eleven were earning a living, while two more were looking for better prospects like a job with fixed tenure or higher income. Only three of the severely disabled girls had never worked or been encouraged to do so either by their families or the NGOs they were in contact with. Disabled women are perceived and represented as dependent and incapable, especially in agro-based rural communities, where they are deemed incapable of contributing to the hard labour required of women. Families devalue and question the girl's ability to engage in productive work like other women, although it depends largely on the degree of impairment and varies greatly depending on available opportunities. Whenever Rita spoke of getting a job, her mother tried to dissuade her, citing her impairment and that she was a woman, as reasons for not working outside the home. Her neighbours would say, 'Why would a disabled girl like you want to work?' Aparna, who helped her father cultivate land, was always told by her father and other villagers that she couldn't work as hard as other women. Aparna accepts such impressions and expresses 'Can I work like a *bhalo manush*' (non-disabled person)? Disabled women themselves internalize such ideas of devaluation and doubt their own abilities. When Mita began looking for a job, she wanted something that was near her home, so that she would not have to travel far. She was unsure about her physical stamina and if she would be able to handle the daily commute to Kolkata and back.

The choice of career is sought to be directed by the male members of the family, as for other girls, and more so in the case of these girls, who are perceived as weak and incapable of hard labour. Manju's father and elder brother wanted her to work as a teacher in a government school, which they felt suited both her disability and her gender. The work considered most apt for women is that of a schoolteacher, as there are fixed hours, minimum travel, a good salary and plenty of holidays. Manju's elder brother promised to help her get a job as a teacher in a government school near their home, as he knew many people in the education department. When she decided to enrol for typing classes, which entailed travelling far every day, her father and elder brother were angry with her. They felt that choosing a secretarial career would entail too much of hard work for a girl like her. Sandhya's father, brother-in-law or brother always check out any place she chooses to work in so that they can ensure her physical safety there. When Mita first got her job, her brother and brother-in-law went with her to ascertain that she would be safe and protected at her workplace.

Girls like Sandhya, Asha, Sulekha and Aparna, living in villages started working from their adolescent years to contribute to the family finances. They had little choice over the work they did or do, taking whatever was available locally and was viable for them. Sulekha, who works for the family business, doesn't like the work because of the heat and the low wages but she is forced to continue because of the money it brings in and also because there are few other alternatives available. Sandhya started work in the refill factory because it was in her village, while Asha has been working from home, embroidering sarees provided by middlemen of the village. Other girls like Mita, Krishna, Manju and Agatha entered the work sphere in order to put their learning to use, prove their worth as well as fill their lives with activity, and live a meaningful life. Krishna changed several jobs before starting her own NGO, which organizes women with disabilities in rural areas to campaign for better services. 'I realized that work would be my life and so I chose to do something I really like.'

Disabled women are found to engage in different kinds of work that entail hard labour, despite the connotations of incapability associated with disability, and weakness associated with both gender and disability. While many of the girls staying in the rural areas work in home-based enterprises and a few travel outside the home to work in the local factories, in the city, disabled girls are working in offices, schools and non-government organizations. However, despite the ideologies regarding their capabilities, disabled women find themselves engaging in hard labour in order to receive a decent income. In the hotel where Anita used to work, she had to help in all the different kinds of chores from cutting vegetables, cleaning and washing the utensils and the tables, helping with the cooking as needed and also serving the food. The utensils were big and heavy and difficult for Anita to manage. While serving food she had to carry buckets full of curry and vegetables to the tables without spilling any of it. Aparna used to work with her father cultivating land that they took on rent. She helped in readying the land by tilling it and breaking the mud into fine soil, sowing the crop and checking for weeds. Later she helped in cutting the crop and binding them in bales and also beating them to de-husk the paddy. Sulekha handles the bulk of the *muri* making for their family business, working from 4 a.m. to 3 p.m. every day, frying the rice and packing it in the sacks. In a day they fry about 160 kg. of rice, with Sulekha working steadily through the day and helped in turns by her mother, sister and sometimes her father.

Most people do not expect disabled girls to be able to fulfil their work responsibilities. Being aware of this impels the girls to take on their jobs as a challenge. Agatha started working in a field-based project of a leading NGO in Kolkata that entailed travelling extensively in the villages. It became a means of proving her capability and equality with other women. Sandhya tries hard to be accepted as one of the workers in the refill factory where she works. She never shirks work because of her impairment, or asks for any special concessions or privileges. Instead of using her disability as an excuse in her workplace, she works as all other women there do. Mita wanted her colleagues to accept her as an equal and not look upon her as weak and *akham* (incapable). 'I wanted to prove that I was as good as or even better than *bhalo manush*.' As supervisor at a residential institution for disabled children, her responsibilities included looking after the needs of the residential children, maintaining relevant records and accounts, planning children's diet as well as disbursing the stocks of linen and clothing. She used to do most of the work herself, getting up early and working till late so that no one would be able to cast aspersion on her.

Sometimes workplaces also offer the women special privileges because of their disability. Manju was allowed to leave 30 minutes before closing time in order to avoid crowded buses of the rush hour. She accepted it and never thought otherwise till a new manager pointed it out to her that she could not avail such privileges as she was a full-time employee and was bound by all the rules regarding employees. Removal of privileges brings about feelings of frustration and helplessness, as Mita experienced at work. She had been assigned a helper for heavy work, like cleaning of the storeroom, where heavy sacks of rice and other foodgrains as well as kitchen and laundry items were kept in huge cupboards. But when the management of the institution changed, Mita's helpers were removed and she was expected and forced to do all the work by herself. 'They (the management) didn't even consider that it would be very difficult for me to do it all by myself.'

Gendered ideologies are used as a threat or punishment to discredit disabled women and prove that they are not *bhalo* (good) women. As supervisor of the junior staff working in the kitchen, Mita had to deal with missing food and linen on a daily basis. If she caught someone stealing and accused them, she had to bear the reprisals from the entire group of staff, who taunted her for being *khoda/langda* and cast aspersions on her femininity. 'As I was unmarried and without children, they even called me barren and incapable of understanding because I had never borne children.' The gender/ability ideologies that deny women without children recognition as women were used by junior staff as a weapon to discredit and devalue Mita, both on grounds of her disability and because she was a woman. Similarly, when the management wanted her to quit the job, they resorted to maligning Mita's reputation as a good woman by insinuating that she was having an affair with one of her married colleagues. The speculation about her relationship and fear of loss of her reputation as a *bhalo meye* compelled Mita to leave her job, thereby reinforcing patriarchal controls over her morality and character as a woman and ableist ideologies about a disabled person as a capable worker.

Anita found work in the cement factory near her house, doing a variety of jobs on contract basis, like making rice by boiling, drying and de-husking paddy for the workers, cutting the grass in the lawns to sweeping the factory premises. She took other women with her to gather firewood and twigs from the factory's premises for cooking, and for sweeping the jetty once a week and cutting the grass in the lawns of the company owning the jetty. But Anita was not allowed to continue there for long, as the other villagers were envious of her contacts in the factory and started spreading rumours about her 'liaisons' inside. 'The villagers talked about how I was granting the factory people sexual favours in order to get the work. They were angry that a *bamun* (short person commonly referred to as 'dwarf') like me was able to find work so easily.' When the village people started to harass the officers in the factory, Anita left the work as she didn't want to be discredited and tagged as a 'loose' immoral woman, destroying her reputation as a *bhalo meye*.

Thus, we can see that women, growing up with a disability, come to accept and negotiate their bodies in accordance with the notions they internalize about their femininity, and experience their embodiment in specifically different ways in comparison to other women. While the ability to, and the manner in which they move, affects the way in which they present a feminine self and participate in the activities labelled as 'feminine', girls themselves seek to express their femininity through the ways in which they dress and behave. While trying to merge the demands of an impaired body with the imperatives of a normative femininity, women adapt and redefine notions of femininity, which is seen as unavailable to them as their sexuality is considered to be frozen at adolescence. Disabled women at the same time also modify accepted feminine practices to suit their needs in their everyday lives. In the realms of sexual division of labour both within the home and outside, the efforts of disabled women are recognized but they are not attributed the capability to cope with the responsibility that is credited to other adult women. In the arena of household work, difference and devaluation is deliberately created in the representation of disabled women's work as *gharer kaaj*, while other adult married women are responsible for the *sansarer kaaj*. In the realm of work, disabled women grapple with ideologies that posit them as incapable and engage in different income generating activities involving hard work, but still end up being represented as incapable and discriminated not only because of their disability but also because of their gender.

Femininity and Sexuality

The chief emphasis of the training of girls for womanhood is on modesty, which is linked with femininity (Cormack 1961). The concept of *lajja* (shyness, modesty) or shame governs and underlies all references to civilized or proper behaviour appropriate to girls and women, which deals with the realms of morals and manners (Bannerji 2002). In adolescence, girls learn the female behavioural norms that impose social strictures on women's visibility, mobility, and behaviour, and impinge directly on their autonomy and ability to participate effectively in public spaces dominated by men (Agarwal 2001). Disabled girls are subjected to the same processes of socialization as their sisters and other women, and have learnt, accepted and internalized notions of modesty, shame, morality, and prescribed norms of behaviour for girls as they step into puberty. Like all other girls in the family and neighbourhood, they, too, are subject to rules of seclusion and avoidance, more so as they pass from childhood to adolescence.

Menstrual processes

Like all other girls, puberty for disabled girls is a process of becoming women. It entails certain rules and restrictions imposed upon their movements as well as proscriptions during menses like being restricted from playing strenuous games, participation in religious ceremonies, restrictions on entering the kitchen, etc. (Bagchi, Guha and Sengupta 1997). In general, mothers, other women in the extended family and friends assume that the disabled girl's pubertal processes would be affected. Agatha remembers her mother telling her, 'a normal girl would have got it by the age of thirteen but you are a different kind of child'. Such comments and ideas make disabled girls more aware of the difference between themselves and other girls, many of them their own sisters, cousins and friends. Few were aware of bodily changes and pubertal processes, and whatever knowledge they gleaned were through secret discussions with friends and sisters. Chobi remembers that her friends 'told me that menses mean that a girl has become a woman. I was told that all girls have it but not why it happened only to girls'. Asha recalls that her cousins had told her that menstruation meant 'bad blood that has to go out of the body'. There is a reluctance to discuss such matters with mothers, due to internalized ideas about shame. 'How could I discuss such a thing with my mother? I was so ashamed. We used to talk about it amongst ourselves, but we never discussed such matters with our mother.'

Many of the girls participating in this study started menstruating much later than their sisters and other girls. Girls are worried about the late onset, as it seems to them another dimension of their difference with other women, and a questioning of their femininity. Asha, the eldest of six sisters started her menses after all her sisters and found it to be extremely embarrassing. 'Everyone used to ask me if my menses had started and it was shameful. All my sisters were getting it every month while mine were not starting at all. Sometimes I used to worry that I would never become a woman.' While delay in menarche leads to frustrations and anxiety about one's femininity, the onset of menstruation is also characterized by fear and worry about negotiation of impairments with the periodic needs of their cycle. Saraswati recalls that when her periods started, she had no idea about it. 'When I saw my pants soaked in blood one day, I was very frightened. No one had told me that it would happen like that.' It was her mother and sister who showed her how to use cloth pads and helped her during those days. Jahanara's first menses started when she was at school and the teachers gave her cloth and taught her how to use it. 'I went home and told my sisters and cousins, but not my mother, as I was feeling ashamed.' Sisters, female cousins and other women directed them in ways of taking care during the menstrual periods.

Ritual practices performed at the onset of menstruation vary between the different castes and communities, but generally include seclusion. This is done to minimize contact with males as a menstruating woman is considered to be polluting (Bhattacharya 1980). The practice of and adherence to these rituals varies from family to family depending not only on caste and community, but also on family type and location of the family and the degree of disability. Mild to moderately disabled girls from rural areas from the lower castes and those from upper castes in urban areas found the rituals more strictly enforced in their lives, as they were equally applicable for all the women of the family. In families that follow rigorous ritual observances at the onset of a girl's menstrual cycle, disabled girls were treated like the other daughters and had to undergo the same ritualistic practices. These practices include separate confinement during the first cycle, taking a bath to purify oneself at the end of the period and undergoing ritualistic puja at the end of it.

Girls are confined to a separate room during their first menstrual cycle for fear of their enhanced sexuality and its polluting nature, and they are directed to have minimal contact with men. Asha was told, 'If you see men during that period, then they will die soon.' Rituals of purification included bathing and washing of the hair and discarding all the clothes used during the 4–5 day confinement. In some families, priests are summoned to do a ritual puja as a cleansing ritual. For Manju, the cleansing bath and ritualistic puja was held on the ghats of the river Hooghly, which was both scary as well as embarrassing for her. 'There was a big puja held at the ghat and everyone came to know that I had started my periods and become a woman. It was so embarrassing. For me, getting into the Ganga with my callipers also was quite difficult. My mother told me to take them off and I was scared I would slip and break my leg on the ghat. Later I was also embarrassed by the fact that I had to sit on the crowded ghat and lift my dress up to my thighs to take off and wear the calliper. But my mother was adamant about the rituals for me too.'

Cloth pads are preferred and girls find the thicker cotton pads more convenient, not just for economic reasons and easy availability but also because it allows them to balance the requirements of their menses with the needs of their impairment. Mita says that she feels comfortable using thick cloth pads because of her weak legs and unstable hips. 'Even though I used to tie a string around my hips to hold it in place, the ready to use pad available in the shops would continuously shift when I walked. I could not manage it properly.' Manju recalls that she used to have more problems during her periods at home as she didn't wear the calliper at home. 'Keeping the home made cloth pad in place was difficult as one of my legs is thin and the muscles don't have much power. Cloth pads are thicker and do not fall out easily or shift fast.'

The mortification associated with the transgressing of feminine bodily norms affects these girls equally. Dora feels bad as her clothes get stained regularly because she is sitting in the wheelchair the whole day. Saraswati prefers to wear a nightgown all day as it helps in reducing staining of her clothes. 'I can also easily lift it up for using the toilet or for changing pads. But during winter, when I wear only salwar kameezes, my clothes get stained.' Agatha recounted the manner in which she dealt with the problem of stained school uniforms in her school days. 'Compared to the other girls, I would be sitting down much more. There was more chance of my dress getting soiled so I learnt to sit with my dress upon the chair. All the girls would do the same.'

The socio-cultural practices with regard to menstruation and the menstrual period decrees that women have to undergo and maintain strict observances, the most common restriction being on touching the *thakurer asan* (seat of the family gods) while having periods. Mita's family was the strictest in terms of ritual observances during the menses. All the sisters would be strictly confined in a particular room when they had their menstrual cycle every month, and all the articles of daily use by them would be kept separate to avoid all contact with the rest of the family. They would sleep on separate beds and rooms for those few days, and when the monthly periods ended, all the clothes, bed sheets, covers, pillow covers and even the mosquito nets used would be thoroughly washed. They were not allowed to touch the pot of rice and other food items and the *thakur ghar* (room of the gods) was completely banned to them. However, they were allowed to do some of the household tasks like cleaning the rooms, washing clothes, cleaning utensils, etc. Over the years, Mita has been able to relax some of the proscriptions and although she still has to sleep in a separate bed and wash all the bed linen and clothes after the periods are over, they are now allowed to enter the kitchen. At Aparna's home, her *ma* enforced only the ritual observance of not touching the *thakurer asan* and barred all the sisters from doing the *sondhye arati*.[3]

For some of the severely disabled girls, mostly living in Kolkata, the proscriptions associated with menstruation were difficult to follow. A certain subversion of the gendered rules surrounding pubertal changes and menstrual avoidance can be seen, probably because of the negation or freezing of the sexuality of disabled women. Dora's father was forced to inform her about and assist her with the process of menstruation, as her mother had left them when she was a baby. He had been worried about the fact that her periods had been delayed and used to ask her openly about it. 'I don't have a mother, so my daddy had to be my mummy also. Once when I was staying with him, he gave me a homeopathic medicine and my periods started soon after. Daddy went and bought sanitary napkins for me.' Chobi, severely disabled and requiring help in all personal care tasks, recalls that although her mother used to help her during her periods, her father used to help her clean up and also change the sanitary pads. 'Initially I used to feel shy but what could I do? I never felt any shame with Baba maybe because he had always been bathing me and taking me to the toilet.' This transgression of norms is probably due to the fact that these girls are seen as frozen in childhood and devoid of sexuality, even though they may be undergoing bodily processes that point to their being a woman.

Girls having orthopaedic disabilities have been experiencing early menopausal symptoms, and are worried about their bodies and health even though some term it as a 'special blessing from God' to lessen their difficulties. Both Asha and Sandhya feel blessed that their periods are so minimal that they are not affected by it at all. Asha says that gods must have felt pity on her for being disabled and said 'let her have fewer problems in life'. Sandhya, who never went to a doctor for irregular menstrual cycles, feels that for disabled girls menstruation is a pain. 'I believe that god has blessed me, as with my disability managing during those days would have been so difficult. God has seen to it that I am rid of those problems and associated aches and pains. Also, it reduces chances of pregnancy just in case.'

Amio ki Meye? *(Am I a woman also?)* *Femininity and Heterosexual Attraction*

The notion of a *bhalo meye* or a physically attractive woman dominates the minds of disabled women as someone who is physically un-impaired, and hence a 'complete' woman. Socialization into socio-cultural ideologies governing lives of women results in internalizing notions of feminine beauty, attractiveness and appropriate feminine behaviour. Patriarchal/ability systems that construct the female norm also specify the visual nature of desirability in women, which for disabled girls, depends not only on the arrangement of their physical features but also on the kind and degree of disability. Girls come to realize that although they are expected to conform to other 'feminine' norms, they are excluded from gendered notions of sexuality. This affects the ways in which disabled girls experience, adapt and deal with culturally valued notions of femininity, desirability and attractiveness. All the girls in the study confessed that they had received messages from society, especially the women around them, all through their childhood and adolescence telling them that they were unattractive to men because of their impairments. While severely disabled girls accepted that social ideologies exclude them from notions of attractiveness, girls with mild and moderate disabilities found it more difficult to accept and negotiate because of the semblance of normality that they had in their lives.

Although in adolescence, with sisters and friends, they discussed boys and what they found attractive in girls, they were scared to reveal their closest feelings regarding men for they feared rejection as women, by both men and women. Krishna confessed that she used to feel anxious about confessing liking for some of the boys they met. 'Even if I liked some boy, I never discussed it with them as I felt they would laugh at me.' Agatha also refused to discuss with her friends about boys whom she liked. 'I feared ridicule for thinking about boys despite being disabled. I used to wonder what they would say if I confessed about a crush.' Their fears have been validated in their interactions with men in the public arena. When disabled girls are sitting with their legs tucked in under them, very few people can make out their impairments, and in such situations, they too are the target of admiring glances and suggestive comments from men. The boys in her locality target Sulekha and her friends with their lewd and suggestive comments, when they are sitting in the pond near their house. Asha related that many time she had been the object of appreciative male attention, in the form of whistles and songs, when she was sitting at the bus stop or in other public places. But Asha is also aware that her attractiveness diminishes once the men realize that she is disabled. 'They look at my legs and say her life is wasted because she can't walk.'

Girls feel that men do not consider them as attractive, as they do not match the feminine requirements of beauty, grace and physical perfection. Mita says that she never received any proposal from boys because she was *khoda* (lame). 'Because I am like this, I am sure no boy ever thought twice about me.' Although Krishna participated in all activities with her friends, she always felt that her male friends were overly protective of her as they 'felt I wouldn't be able to manage because of my disability'. Agatha felt that the boys in her class were 'very careful' with her, took care of her and ensured that she faced few difficulties while walking or sitting, but were always careful to draw a line between her and her other girlfriends. 'They would say don't go by bus, we will take you or we will meet you at such a time, don't go home alone, etc. I received the tender gloves treatment but wasn't considered as proper girlfriend material.' While she was a good friend to them, she feels sad that she was never considered as anything more.

During adolescence, norms of appropriate behaviour that influence lives of all girls are also extended to disabled girls, curbing their freedom to roam freely due to fears of losing their reputation as a '*bhalo meye*'. Mita recalls that her parents wouldn't let her and her sisters go out of the house as they grew older and it was not seemly for them to wander on the roads. However, there is a denial of sexuality when mothers opine that their disabled daughter is less at risk as compared to the non-disabled ones. Asha's mother is less afraid for her older (disabled) daughter than for her younger daughter as she is sure that nothing untoward would happen to Asha. She feels safe enough to leave Asha alone at home till late at night, but worries about her younger daughter in similar circumstances. On the other hand, mothers also asked their disabled daughters to avoid male attention in order to protect their reputation as the onus was on the disabled women, as single women, to guard against getting an unsavoury reputation. Asha's mother felt, 'It is easy to discredit us. If some boy forces his attention on her, everyone will say, she couldn't control herself.' Sulekha's mother urged Sulekha not to incite or excite the local boys, who used to heckle her. '*Ma* says ignore what they are saying as they are like dogs and will stop barking after some time. I know it is my fate and I have to listen to such things.'

Disabled girls also fear both the reputation of a loose woman as well as the shame associated with a disabled woman having sexual urges. This kind of fear of social shame and ostracism, however, was more visible in girls living in rural areas, as these are relatively closed communities, where every action is noticed and commented upon. Sandhya revealed that she has consciously never allowed any man to get close to her. Although she talks to other men in the neighbourhood or in the village, she maintains a distance so that people around them will never get a chance to gossip about her. 'How can I? Just imagine, people would say, "she is like that and look, how she is flirting with boys".' Asha confirmed that she felt scared whenever she talked with men and boys, because rumours about her liaisons with men would ruin her reputation in the village. Asha's mother elaborated, 'what will happen if my disabled daughter's reputation is maligned?' The onus of maintaining their reputation as *bhalo meye* in the moral sense is doubly important for disabled women, as they feel that they already have lost status as a physically and functionally perfect woman. Despite the denial of their sexuality, disabled women fear repercussions, both physical and social, over any sexual attention that they might receive.

Marriageability: Not the Bhalo Meye

The prevalent system for marriage alliances in Bengal, as in the rest of India, is that of arranged marriages, in which parents of the prospective groom and bride seek a suitable match for their son/daughter based on different criteria, of which caste and class are the most important. As the girl child is seen as a sapling to be transplanted as soon as possible from the natal home (Bagchi 1995), proposals for marriage are sought from eligible families and grooms as soon as the girl reaches an age where she is considered ready for marriage.

This stage varies from family to family and from rural to urban settings, although the necessity of marriage for girls is taken for granted. In the process of selection of a bride, families of a groom judge the merits of the girl, a *bhalo meye* from her physical beauty and capabilities, to her other accomplishments and skills. In arranged marriages, the examination of the prospective bride involves her physical appearance such as skin colour, hair, facial features, etc. as well as her skills. Girls are asked to speak, walk, read and write as well as demonstrate other skills to judge her abilities, physical beauty and to ascertain that she doesn't have any deformity or disability (Engels 1996).

Socio-cultural ideologies however, construct disabled women as unsuitable for marriage, and from their adolescence, girls are given subtle messages and come to accept the impossibility of the idea of their marriage. While families rarely tell the girl directly, silences convey the message that she is not considered marriageable, equally loudly. Asha recalls that at her home, no one ever talked of her marriage even though she was the oldest of the sisters. Asha's grandmother would tell her, 'You stay in this house like a son. Other girls will get married and leave but you will stay here always. My mother also says I am like her son as I will never leave home. I am their elder son and my brother, their younger son.' Subtle messages are used to condition the young disabled girl to accept her 'fate' by comparing her to the sons of the family who never have to leave their natal home. The de-sexing of girls is evident in the analogy of the disabled girl being like a son, denying her femininity and sexuality and at the same time underlining the fact that she would never be married off like her other sisters. Manju's female relatives used to commiserate with her mother, 'they would all tell *ma* "you will never have a younger son-in-law"'. Manju later realized that it was a way of sending implicit messages and cautioning her to curtail her own aspirations. Rita recalls that the women in their neighbourhood would repeat, '"*bhalo*" (non-disabled) girls can expect a lot of things and have lots of *sokh* (aspirations, desires), which is not allowed for disabled girls'.

The notion of the *bhalo meye*, a woman who is physically unimpaired, beautiful and capable of physical labour, plays an important role in the representation of disabled women as un-marriageable. The association of marriage for a woman with the ability to engage in household work was foremost in the minds of people in the neighbourhood, who used to ask Asha's father 'Who will marry her? She cannot walk, how will she manage the household work?' Families, people in the community and the girls themselves accept that the nature of their impairments would make it impossible for them to assume responsibility for an entire family and perform all the tasks expected of a married woman.

For girls with impairments, functional capacity becomes one of the primary reasons for not being considered as fit for marriage. Inability to cope with household work and caring for the affinal family are the most common reasons cited for the lack of marriage prospects for disabled women. Sandhya's sister elaborated, 'Which boy will be able to feed her if she is not able to contribute to the *sansarer kaaj*? Who will feed her just like that, without doing any work? How will she be able to do the *sansarer kaaj*?' Girls and their families also fear that their disabled daughter would be subjected to physical violence for not being able to cope with the responsibilities of marriage. Anita's mother opined that, '*bhalo* girls are beaten up by their husbands and in-laws, and deserted. My disabled daughter would be treated worse if she got married'.

Media images of desirable, perfect and marriageable women relegate disabled women to the realms of women not fit for consideration for marriage, as is illustrated by the matrimonial advertisements in the newspapers. Agatha says that from an early age, she had been looking at those advertisements, which look for 'tall, fair, beautiful girls', and over the years, came to realize and accept that she would never fall into the category of a 'beautiful' girl. 'I have learnt that men always look for someone who is perfect. They will not look at girls like me who are less than perfect or who are not "normal". It's not that I am imperfect, but I am not what most men think of as perfect.'

However, aspirations regarding marriage vary with age as well as severity of disability. From her adolescence, Sandhya has always known that marriage was an impossible proposition for her. 'How could they (parents) have even dared to think of my marriage?' Asha felt that, 'they (parents) knew it was of no use thinking about my marriage. I have no legs (meaning that she cannot walk). How could I get married? Everyone knows that girls like me won't be able to do most of the work. Then what will they gain by taking me to their home?' As they grow older, girls with moderate to severe disabilities reconcile themselves to the fact of remaining single throughout their lives. Older girls express fears of being deserted by men after marriage, especially if they were persuaded with the promise of dowry. Asha feels that men may agree to marry her in return for a huge *pon*,[4] but knows that there is no guarantee that he would stay with her. Younger girls are still struggling against societal and familial ideologies that deem that they cannot get married. Sulekha's older and younger sisters have been married off by her parents, who are now looking for a suitable match for their son. Sulekha's mother justified their actions, 'my other daughters were growing up so fast that I did not dare to keep them in my house'. Sulekha feels a bit disappointed that her parents are not thinking of her marriage at all. 'If I could walk like other girls, then my marriage would be considered before my brother's or sister's marriage.'

Notions of social acceptability dominate the minds of disabled girls when it comes to marriage, and the public ramifications of the relationship is given more importance by girls socialized into denying or concealing their sexual needs. The girls emphasize the fulfilment of the desires of their husbands and speculate about the public shame and rejection that their men would face for having a disabled wife. Asha felt that if she were married, she would always be conscious of how her husband would be feeling whenever they went outside the home. She feels that her husband would be embarrassed to accompany her in public places. 'Like when there is some social function either at our home or in other places, he may like me to go with him. How will he take me? Will he walk there and I will crawl beside him? Will he carry me on his shoulders? People would stare and pass comments. Will any man like to have a wife like me?' The fear of social ridicule works in the reverse manner also, when girls with mild to moderate disabilities contemplate marriage with a disabled man. Mita who received a proposal from one of her severely disabled friends decided not to marry him because they would not 'look good together'. She also felt that when they went out, people would stare at them, as her husband would be crawling while she walked beside him. However, she was not averse to marrying a man with a mild to moderate impairment as the visual impact of such a disability is much less than that of a severely disabled man.

Fears regarding their capacity to bear and rear children also dominate the minds of disabled women and their mothers. Asha's mother felt, 'would she be able to perform all the responsibilities of a mother when she cannot even walk?' Asha echoed her mother's fear and expressed her apprehensions that she would not be able to care and provide for her child or even indulge him/her. 'If I have children, the child may want his/her mother to go around with him/her, carry him/her. I cannot fulfil those wishes. I can take him/her on my lap but will not be able to soothe him/her or rock him/her by pacing up and down.'

However, despite such ideologies and fears expressed by the girls and their families, their mothers felt the need to at least try and arrange marriages for their disabled daughter in order to ensure social respectability. Rita's mother felt that her daughter's single status was a constant source of pain for her. 'If someone married her then the label of spinster will be erased.' For women with mild disabilities, marriage is preferred rather than incurring the stigma of being *aiburo* (unmarried girl who has reached puberty). Manju recalls that, when she was young, 'remaining unmarried would have meant that people would comment on it regularly'. An elderly lady living near Asha's home tells her to get married, if only to a token husband like the moon.

Proposals for marriage were received only by the girls with mild to moderate disabilities, with the pre-condition that the groom should be a disabled man himself, as he would probably be the only one willing to marry such a woman. Mita says that for a long time she too, felt and accepted such ideas, as she 'felt that adjustment would be better as we would understand each other's flaws'. Manju's relatives used to advise her father to look for a disabled boy for her, as they were doubtful if any normal boy would prefer to marry her. At that time, Manju didn't think that to be a problem 'as I felt that I deserved such only'. Disabled girls themselves, however, prefer to have non-disabled partners, if possible. The ideas of social acceptability is internalized by them too, and they prefer men, who will be able to 'support' them financially and whose impairment is not visibly severe. Mita remembers that when she was in college, a disabled man working in the railways, proposed marriage. Mita refused because at that time she hoped for a man who was not disabled. Manju recalls that even though she received a proposal from a boy from a higher caste than hers, she had apprehensions about their future life as he had lost one leg in an accident. 'Although he earned a decent living through tuitions, I was sad when the proposal came. I was like this and he also had lost a leg.'

Reactions of parents to such proposals from disabled men vary from family to family. While Mita's parents had steadily refused to entertain any such proposals, Manju's parents would judge the groom on his merits and ability to 'keep' their daughter in financial and physical security. When she was 14 years old, Aparna's parents received a proposal for her from the family of a young man with speech and hearing impairments, who felt that it would be a good match as both were disabled even though Aparna was 'dark and ordinary to look at'. Aparna's mother was very happy with the proposal as she felt that a 'good' boy would ask for a huge dowry for marrying a disabled girl. With four other daughters to marry off, she felt that this was a good match, but her father refused to marry off his disabled daughter to a disabled man. Aparna's mother had argued with him, 'Where will you get a prince to marry your lame daughter?' Aparna also recalls being horrified at the prospect of marrying a disabled man, and was relieved when her *baba* refused the proposal.

Offers of marriage from non-disabled men come with clauses and conditions attached to them. When Anita was 22 years old, a boy, originally from the Sundarbans, but working near to her house, approached her family for marrying her. The boy's only request was to stay as *ghar jamai* (practice of husband moving to live with wife's family) with a 'good' girl as he had no family left. He didn't have any objections to marrying a disabled girl if his pre-condition was fulfilled. When Anita's parents met him to finalize the marriage, the boy demanded land as dowry to build a house for both of them to stay. When his demand was refused, he left saying he didn't have the means to support Anita after marriage. 'He would have accepted a disabled wife only with the lure of property as dowry.' Manju received a proposal from a 'well-qualified' man living with his brother and sister-in-law, but when they saw her, they asked for a piece of land as *pon*. 'They could think of marriage with me only if the *pon* was sizeable enough.'

Thus, the social processes whereby the disabled girls become and learn to behave like women actively work towards denying and suppressing their sexuality and growing feelings regarding their femininity and desirability.

Bodily processes like menstruation enable them to claim status as women, but are also experienced as problematic as the management during the period needs to take into consideration the bodily difference. Their similarity with their sisters is proved not only by the mandatory onset of menarche but also by the family's imposition of proscriptive rules and rituals which all women have to undergo during the period. However, celebrating unity with women around them is balanced by the accentuation of the difference with other women especially when it comes to desirability and marriageability. Disabled girls feel that, judged against the imaginary norm of femininity and the ideal *bhalo meye*, they are found wanting in all relationships that allow women to express their sexuality. Ideologies of feminine attractiveness represent impaired bodies and disabled women as undesirable, unfit for attracting the attention of possible partners and incapable of entering relationships that require women to assume roles of wife, mother and carer for the family members. The encounters that these women have had with men in the public sphere have reaffirmed these beliefs and representations, with rejection and negation of their femininity being the primary responses. Marriage, as an option, was one of the last considerations for disabled girls and proposals, solicited at later ages compared to their sisters, were received mainly from disabled men, reinforcing notions of devaluation as women.

In the Public Domain: Accentuating the Difference

Beyond the family, in the neighbourhoods and kinship networks, identities of disabled women are further strengthened, ratified, questioned, debated and modified in accordance with the dominant gender/ability ideologies. In the public domain, girls are more openly confronted with dominant ideas regarding femininity and ability and stereotypical representations that cast them as dependent, incapable and weak. Within the neighbourhood, despite evidence of the work that they engage in on a daily basis, women are subjected to comments like *or pa kharap* (legs are bad meaning non-functional) or *kaajkorte pare na* (cannot do any work). Seeing them in the public domain amounts to a transgression of norms of acceptability, which is both gendered and ability centred. Aparna's neighbours and some of the people from her village expressed that disabled people should not aspire to venture far from home or attempt to engage in activities that able-bodied people take for granted. Later, Aparna explained that some of these men were contemptuous of her attempts to grow crops and frowned upon her visits to the NGO. In Chauli village, the member of the Panchayat burst out, 'Every month she goes to some meeting. What is the need to go so far? She has to depend on her family for taking her to the main road . . . what is so important that a disabled girl like her has to go to such meetings?' Asha recalls that whenever she went to the bi-annual video shows held in her village, 'Many people would say why do you come with so much trouble? I used to feel then, why can't I also have *sokh-sadh* (desire/aspiration/wish)? Just because I cannot walk?'

Dora, who has been in a wheelchair all her life, used to feel demeaned every time she went to public places, as people around her would always be commenting about her. 'Some people even said, what's the use of her living?' Living and dealing with pity and ridicule on a daily basis makes the girls more aware of their differences with other women, and the fact that compared to non-disabled women they are found to be wanting. Whenever Asha goes out in public transport, people make her feel as if there is nothing as bad as a disabled woman. 'People say, "oh what a sad thing to happen, if only god had not taken away both legs, if only she could walk, what a punishment for such a beautiful girl". It was as if all my beauty would now be wasted as I cannot walk.'

The realization of difference, of being distinctive so much so that they become the cynosure of all eyes in the public domain, and of debasement, has been the general experience of disabled girls whenever they have ventured out into the public sphere. The degree of disability or the visual impact of one's impairment determines the kind of attention one gets, feels Sulekha, who has been aware all her life that people stare at her. 'But if I go out of the house crawling, instead of with the callipers, more people would stare at me.' When she is walking with her callipers, she feels that people stare at her but there is less pity in their eyes than when she is crawling along the road. Agatha has developed a thick skin and different strategies of ignoring unwanted attention and processes of objectification in public spaces. Initially she used to stare back at them, but over the years she has realized that they stare because they have not seen many disabled people in the public arena.

In the public spaces, girls also have to reckon with the way in which people react to them and also how they use derogatory language to refer to them. The most common terms used to describe them are *khudi* or *pratibandhi meye* (disabled girl) and these are used in pitiful or disdaining tones. When Asha crawls along with her family, people often say to them, 'Can't you carry her? Why does she have to crawl?' Asha feels that people want to see women like her being dependent on others and hence they cannot understand her wanting to move independently. When she goes to board a vehicle, co-passengers wanting to help her grab her arms, not realizing that her hands are her legs and if they hold her arms she will not be able to move at all. Mita clarified, 'the implication is always that as we are weak in society so our anger and frustration is always more. That disabled people may also have an opinion and that they may also be allowed to do or say things they like, is unacceptable.'

Prevalent ideologies posit them as 'incomplete' women, who do not need any form of ornamentation or dressing up as against 'normal' women, who have to adhere to acceptable notions of femininity. Manju recalls that when she was in college, if she dressed up and went out, boys would invariably taunt her, '"She can't walk properly yet see how she dresses up." As if disabled girls have no right to dress up. So I also started feeling that I shouldn't dress up or put on makeup to make myself pretty. I refused to wear sarees, as they made me look more feminine.' Disabled women, considered to be unfeminine and unattractive, are relegated to the side lines of femininity and hence need not attempt to beautify themselves as objects of male pleasure. Krishna, who travels regularly by bus, often has to hear derogatory comments about being 'overdressed'. 'One day, in a crowded bus, when I got a seat, I bent down to release the knee-lock of my calliper. I like to wear long dangling earrings and these were jangling as I struggled with the task. One man said to the other, "Look at her, disabled and yet so dressed up!"'

Krishna feels the male-centric society defines notions of femininity and acceptability according to conventional ideas of beauty. According to her, men stare at her and pass comments not only because she is disabled, but also because despite being disabled, she wears unconventional or non-traditional trendy clothes like jeans and blouses. 'I feel if I conformed in dress code and did not wear jewellery or ostentatious makeup, people would find it easier to accept my disability. People want disabled women to be conformist. Maybe if I wore a saree then I would receive lesser comments.' Sandhya has been made to accept over the years that village people do not prefer to see her 'all dressed up'. 'People in the village don't want to see a disabled girl dressed up and if I wear good clothes or jewellery they will say, "See the disabled girl, dressed up like a heroine". They say many things like, "See how she is and so much of desire to dress up".'

Disabled women face both a denial of their sexuality as well as sexual abuse in the public domain. Men in public spaces often treat these women as available for not only ridicule and pity but also for sexual favours. The ideology that deems these women as sexually unattractive works in the favour of men who treat disabled women as objects of pleasure without fear of repercussions, as 'who would ever think of doing anything to a girl like her?' Anita feels sad when her sexuality is denied by men who deem her unfit for marriage, while making sexually suggestive comments when they meet her in social situations. Even some of her *gyati* (blood-kin) men and brothers-in-law tease her with sexually loaded comments and invite her alone to watch movies or go out for pleasure. 'Don't I know what they want? I have to be very careful, because I am a woman.' Anita feels they think that because she is short, she also must be less intelligent. 'Some jokingly offer to marry me, and others refer to me as their *chotobou* (younger wife, with the connotation of short or small wife). I feel sad, because I know they would never dare to crack such jokes with other women, yet they laugh loudly at me.' Anita knows that if she complains, very few people would believe that she had been treated as a sexual object while others would feel that she invited the comments in some way.

During social occasions and festivals, the creation and realization of difference is somehow intensified with disabled women finding it difficult to manoeuvre through crowded places and the 'gaze' of so many people at the same time. Sandhya rarely attends any marriage ceremonies held in her village ostensibly because of her mobility problems. Although she feels ashamed at having to crawl in or be carried, she also feels self-conscious of her impairment as people stare at her constantly. The 'gaze' for disabled girls is constituted not just by the way men look at and objectify women, but also by the way in which the non-disabled world looks at disabled people. Hence, they feel the simultaneous pressures of the feminine and able-bodied bodily norms, especially in varied social situations, where they feel the gaze constantly assessing and demeaning them. In Bengal, Durga Puja is usually celebrated in a communal manner and crowds of people throng to the *puja* pandal to offer prayers and marvel at the idols of the goddess. Disabled girls prefer to avoid such crowded pandals,[5] not only because it is inconvenient for them to navigate with their mobility aids, but mostly because of the 'gaze', the way non-disabled people look and stare at them. Sulekha says that she prefers not to go out for Durga Puja, mainly because of the crowds, as she can't walk fast or rush forward as fast as the other people. She feels that her sisters or friends who accompany her find it difficult to walk slowly with her and often get irritated and impatient. Moreover, she is bothered by pitiful, sympathetic and mocking comments that focus only on her impairment. Saraswati, who was taken by the NGO to see Durga *thakur* (idols of Goddess Durga) in Kolkata, finds comfort and anonymity in that group. 'I go in a wheelchair and maybe people also stare at me, but I don't mind their stares so much as I don't know them.' She hardly ever visits the puja held near to her house, as 'Instead of seeing the *thakur*, people will look at me and I don't like it.'

Government systems are characterized by apathy towards disabled women, whether it is the transport systems of the local administration. Disabled girls feel that the transport system in West Bengal is most unresponsive to the needs of disabled people, with the buses being inaccessible and the staff rude and indifferent. Agatha explained that the government or the local transport companies never feel that disabled people will be using their services. The government ruling, as per the PWD Act 1995, to provide free transport or concessions to disabled people in all state run transport, acts against them as bus operators feel that to take such passengers will be to deprive paying passengers. Hence, most buses in Bengal, public or private, deliberately refuse to carry disabled people, and will not stop at the space marked for a bus stop or for long enough for the disabled people to get on, knowing fully well that they will not be able to walk fast enough or get into the bus quickly like other people. This is despite the fact that most of these girls travel in buses run by private operators (as government buses do not ply in routes near their homes) and have to pay the full fare.

Girls feel that the rude behaviour of the bus drivers and conductors mirror the hostile state and social attitudes towards them. Rita said that some times when she gets in to a bus, she has to hear comments like, 'now a disabled person is in the bus, the entire day will prove unlucky'. Conductors behave rudely, intimidating them and hassling them in different ways. In the bus, there are two seats at the back reserved for disabled people, but these are the most uncomfortable seats in the bus. There is very little leg space, and many disabled people who wear callipers find it difficult to position their legs properly. If the girls sit on seats reserved for women, the conductors shout at them as they are filling up the seats of the paying passengers. Manju says very few buses actually provide a free ride, and conductors who know that she pays her fare regularly, often behave rudely too. 'They shout to one another, "don't take her, she will not pay her fare". It is so embarrassing, even though I always pay the full fare.'

Government departments and local government offices discriminate openly against disabled girls, and gender here plays an important role in the way in which the access to schemes and programmes is conditioned. They are treated as women and dependent on men, rather than disabled women who might seek to be independent. When Asha applied for a loan to the local panchayat to start her own business, she was told that she is not eligible, as she is earning a living and is still with her parents, and so she doesn't really need the money. Requests for better roads also have fallen on deaf ears of the political leaders, who appear only during elections and disappear even faster. In Sandhya's panchayat office, she has applied many times for either a tricycle or for loans and jobs. 'They said "why should we help you with a loan? Your brothers are working, why ask for help?" So what if my brothers are working? How does that help me? They don't support me or give me anything. They don't care for me or even look after me.'

The cultural meanings attributed to different bodies has a great impact on formation of identities that are gendered yet coloured by ableist ideologies. For women with disabilities, the body becomes the sole point of both similarity and difference between them and other women, and determine the ways in which they perceive and experience the difference in everyday lives. Disabled women strive to adhere, as far as possible, to the socially acceptable ideas about a *bhalo meye* through different strategies of presenting a feminine self, in gait and bearing, in dress and comportment and through activities and practices. Normative femininity is accepted and endorsed, and negotiated with the ramifications of their impairments. An embodiment that is shaped by an impaired body coupled with the socio-cultural valuation of a disabled person as well as of the different social roles a woman plays, greatly influences the way in which a disabled femininity is constructed, nurtured and contested. These women also redefine the ideal of a *bhalo meye* in the different domains of their daily lives, whether in the private realms of their homes and personal processes or in the public sphere. The creation of differences, based on the material reality of their impairment as well as assumed preconceptions about their capabilities, leads them to accept their impaired bodies as something which is devalued and 'wanting' as compared to other women. However, in daily practice, the impaired body engages in and manages almost all of the activities and practices that govern daily lives of these women, although this may vary according to the degree of disability. Disabled women redefine norms according to the imperatives of their impairments and this is viewed by family and community in a paternalistic manner, where the modified behaviour is accepted on the condition that expressions of sexuality and femininity are overtly rejected. In other domains, especially in terms of sexual division of labour within and outside the home, disability is thrust upon them, in the form of ideas regarding work appropriate for women who are considered to have reduced physical capacities. This is most profoundly realized in the way disabled women are represented as engaging in *gharer kaaj* while other 'normal' women are seen to assume the responsibility for *sansarer kaaj*.

The sexual female body is celebrated as it signifies that the girl has become a woman with the promise of productive and reproductive capabilities. For disabled women, becoming a woman or the onset of menarche is a signal of her potential femininity, despite the difficulties they face in managing the monthly periods. However, the celebration of unity with other women is counteracted by cultural constructions that produce the female body as desirable and attractive and capable of fulfilling both productive and reproductive functions, which are deemed as the most important responsibilities for a woman. Feminine beauty norms find impaired female bodies lacking and confer on it ideologies of incapacity and unattractiveness in sexual and other relationships. The process of negation and denial of the sexuality of disabled women proceeds from suppression within the household to encounters in the public sphere, that serve to reinforce the ideologies and lead to withdrawal of disabled women, sometimes reluctantly, from the arena of sexuality. But this process varies according to the degree of disability as well as the family contexts in which the girls are located and the aspirations they were allowed to harbour from adolescence into adulthood.

In the public sphere, disabled girls feel most conscious of their impaired bodies and realize their failure to live up to the expectations from female bodies. Interactions outside the home whether in the neighbourhood or in the wider social spaces almost always reinforce the differences and highlight the deficiencies of the impaired feminine body. The realization that their bodies are different from the socially constructed physical norm impels disabled women to draw as little attention as possible while they negotiate public spaces. Yet they find themselves at the centre of focus in their public encounters, with people focusing only on their impairments and ignoring their presence as women. Moreover, these stigmatizing encounters also convey messages about the ways in which disabled female bodies rouse public sympathy but are rejected and discriminated against not only because they are disabled but also because they are female. The 'gaze' constructs and devalues impaired female bodies that occupy public spaces and pushes them further into the margins of society.

Notes

1. Durga Puja (Worship of Durga), also referred to as Durgotsava (Festival of Durga) or Sharadotsav, is an annual Hindu festival in South Asia that celebrates worship of the Hindu Goddess Durga. The festival marks the victory of Goddess Durga over the evil buffalo demon Mahishasura. Thus, it epitomizes the victory of good over evil. The pujas are held over a ten-day period, which is traditionally viewed as the coming of the married daughter, Durga, to her father, Himalaya's home. It is the most important festival in Bengal, and Bengalis celebrate with new clothes and other gifts, which are worn on the evenings when the family goes out to see the 'pandals'.
2. A pandal is fabricated structure, either temporary or permanent, used for religious ceremonies, especially to venerate the goddess Durga during Durga Puja, known as puja pandal.
3. Evening ritual of lighting a lamp in front of the seat of the gods and then taking it to all other rooms of the house.
4. Dowry paid at the time of marriage in form of gifts and gold jewellery.
5. Makeshift structure made of bamboo and covered with cloth used popularly for community worship/festivals.

CHAPTER VI

Changing Family Relationships Adulthood

'My biggest angst is that I am a girl'

Adulthood is a very significant stage in the life of a disabled woman, because her experiences of the social world and perceptions about herself undergo change and are redefined both by herself and by the people around her. A disabled woman experiences complex social relationships throughout her adult life within the natal family as a single woman and in her affinal family as the married woman, wife and mother. The boundaries between adolescence and adulthood blur in some of the experiences the girls face during the course of their lives. Often affective relationships are forged by the disabled women in accordance with or challenging the normative construction of their identities as disabled women living in families. Over time, the relationships disabled women have with the men as well as the women within the natal family, change. She negotiates and shapes her experiences of the social world around her and engages in relationships that are distinctive yet different in quality.

Married women with disabilities go through different experiences in the course of their marriage; in the *sasurbari* as a *natun bou* (new bride), in the relationships with her in-laws and her husband and then in the process of becoming a mother. Be it the natal or the affinal family, there are different ways in which gender and disability structure influence and compels her to redefine the relationships and her experiences in them, in order to be a woman.

The Natal Family

Relationships of a woman with the natal family undergo change over time; more so as she grows up. As a girl considered to be a sapling to be transplanted at the time of marriage (Bagchi 1995), the natal home is

* Certain sections of this chapter have been published in *Economic and Political Weekly*, vol. XLV, no. 17, April 2010 and as part of a chapter in an edited volume entitled *Disability Studies in India*, ed. Renu Adlakha, New Delhi, 2013.

treated as a temporary place where she learns to behave as a woman and is trained in the skills most necessary for her future roles as wife and mother. Hence, fathers are usually indulgent of their daughters, who they perceive will leave the natal home and then come back only occasionally for visits. Within the Bengali home and in most Indian families, girls usually share a close affectionate bond with their father (Roy 1972), who loves and spoils them, while mothers usually discipline their daughters and train them for their future roles in life. Disabled girls, who remain unmarried and continue to live within the natal home, perceive a change in the relationships they share with their fathers and mothers once they reach adulthood. For disabled girls, the affectionate relationship that they share with their fathers continues into adulthood, though the relationship becomes a little distanced because of cultural norms that proscribe close physical contact with adult daughters. Some daughters continue to be cosseted by their fathers, mostly because of a feeling of injustice for the daughter who has been denied a woman's life. Asha's father, who stays away from home due to work pressure and comes home once a week, always brings a token gift for her. 'My other daughters get a lot from life, go to different places. But what enjoyment does Asha have in her life?'

Mothers become the main support system for the disabled girls as their sisters get married and move away. The girls build a close rapport with their mothers who look after their personal care, especially for severely disabled girls, and share a companionship of being women responsible for the family. Mothers and disabled daughters form a mutual support system, sharing joys and sorrows, successes and frustrations. Most of Asha's day is spent in the company of her mother, talking, arguing, and helping each other in work. Asha's mother compares Asha to her *sasuri*, for being with her all the time, nagging her about different things, asking her to do things for her and being at home all the time. Although they argue over some issues, the love that they share is evident from their interactions and from the stories they tell. If Asha goes anywhere, even to visit her married sisters, her mother misses her terribly and doesn't relax until she is home.

Girls share a close bond with their younger sisters, female cousins and the few friends remaining in the neighbourhood. Sisters, as yet unmarried, help them with everything in which they need assistance, ranging from personal care and buying necessities to helping with work-related activities. Agatha's closest friend had been her younger sister, till she moved away first for her studies and then for work. Saraswati, who needs help with most of her personal care tasks, was heavily dependent on her younger sister for assistance. Disabled girls often need help with trivial tasks like putting the washed clothes on the line for drying, although they may be performing most of their personal and household responsibilities. Asha's sister helps her whenever she has to go out, either the monthly visit to the NGO or to visit her sisters, carrying her on the cycle up to the main road from where she has to catch a bus. However, these women also share an envious and sometimes antagonistic relationship with their able-bodied sisters, because they realize that as disabled women, they will never be seen as *bhalo meye* in terms of marriage, while their sisters conform to the accepted notions of femininity. Saraswati refused to share any of her clothes and jewellery with her sister, although her younger sister allowed her to use all her belongings. Sometimes her sister would request Saraswati to let share her room, but she always rejected such proposals. 'I always told her that I didn't like other people in the room. If she asked me to share my things with her, I used to tell her I don't want to take from you nor do I want to give to you. I was jealous because she could walk and meet other people, while I remained at home.'

In most families while the sons are privileged and enjoy special benefits and advantages, disabled girls are also accorded special status in the family. However in adulthood, the disabled daughter finds her position within the home undergoing enormous transformation. After a protected and pampered upbringing, she finds herself being treated as an adult, who is deemed dependent yet expected to take responsibility for household work. In poorer families living in the rural areas, disabled girls are forced to participate in the sexual division of labour within and outside the home, propelled by the financial needs of the family. Sulekha, who works long hours making puffed rice, complained that her elder brother only has to fetch the rice and deliver the puffed rice to the local businessmen, and can decide about the spending of their family income. As a son, her brother is definitely more valued and cherished within the home than Sulekha, who is forced to do work she doesn't like because she is an unmarried girl living with her parents and perceived as dependent. Sandhya feels let down by her brothers, who did not stop her from moving away from home to earn a living. 'I thought that my brothers would at least say, "Don't go. It doesn't seem nice that you being a disabled girl are going to work away from the home." Here people tell my sister, "How can your brothers let your disabled sister work?"' Sandhya, who stays with her elder sister at her in-laws' home, feels ashamed of her brothers, who were portrayed as her providers and protectors. 'None of my brothers cared enough for me to tell me to stay back at home.'

Married Brothers and their Families

Within a patriarchal culture, sons are claimants of privileged status within the household because they are seen as the ones to continue the lineage and are, thus, the rightful heirs of property. In such a context, single disabled girls, though living with the natal family and considered as sons, are still denied the advantages accorded to her brothers. In adulthood, an unmarried disabled girl living in the natal home finds herself in a precarious situation, where her parents and society deem her a full member of the family and yet treat her as ancillary to the natal household. Her presence in the natal home announces not only her single status but it also has the power to cast a shadow over future relationships to be forged through marriage for her siblings. Both Asha's and Sulekha's parents were afraid that they would not be able to get good husbands for their other daughters because of the presence of their disabled daughter in their home. Asha, the oldest, feels lucky that none of her sisters were rejected because of her. She feels that men looking for brides are not bothered by a disabled sister-in-law, as they will take the bride away from her natal home and will not have to take responsibility for or care for the disabled sister. However, disabled girls felt that they were a liability for their family when it came to the question of marriage of their brothers. The *ghatak* (marriage negotiator) contacted by Sulekha's parents to find a bride for their son told them that 'some families may have a problem in marrying their daughter in a house where there is a disabled *nanad* (husband's sister)'. Sandhya remembers that one girl's family rejected her brother as a groom because they had seen her when they came to visit. 'They said there is a lame sister-in-law there, so we will not marry our daughter into your family.' After that, Sandhya used to hide when the marriage negotiations for any of her siblings was going on. 'What if the marriage negotiations are again cancelled because of me?'

The gender order of Bengal deems that a woman's marital home is her 'real' home, and daughters are privileged but temporary residents at their father's home until the time they get married and move away. As brothers grow up and increasingly take over the responsibility of the household, the power dynamics within the household shifts from the older parents to the younger men and the women they marry. As there are no aspirations or models associated with spinsterhood in Bengali society (Östör and Fruzzetti 1982), within the home, an unmarried girl has lesser value in comparison to the women who marry into the family. With the coming of the *boudi* (elder brother's wife), disabled girls feel that their brothers distanced themselves and concentrated more on their wives and children. Disabled woman, with few prospects of marriage, were relegated to secondary position on the arrival of the *boudi*, who enjoys greater prestige and privilege in the family not just because she is married but also because she is 'normal'. A 'normal' (non-disabled) married woman achieves adulthood upon marriage and is valued more as she is seen as capable of managing all the *sansarer kaaj* and household responsibilities, while the unmarried disabled woman is considered to be frozen in childhood and incapable of dealing with the *sansarer kaaj*.

Within the natal home, coexistence with the *boudis* is dependent both on the girl's own position in the family as well as the *boudis*' ability to accept and adjust to an unmarried disabled *nanad*. Disabled girls accept the socio-cultural ideologies regarding their status in the natal home and negotiate with their *boudis* to establish a cordial relationship with their married brothers and their wives. This is especially true of those girls who are able to help with the household work, and those who are earning a living. Being able to contribute to the household, whether by sharing household chores or financially, gives them a stronger position to negotiate their relationship with the new women in the family. Sandhya feels that as she is out of the house a lot and as her income makes her less dependent on her brothers, her *boudis* or *bhai bou* (wife of younger brother) treat her nicely. As she goes out to work, there is little scope of friction with her *boudis* for control over the household and the attention of the brother/husband. The fact that these women are earning their living and contributing to family expenses, and hence less dependent on their brothers, also affects the equations between the women in economically disadvantaged families living in rural areas. The coming of *boudis* releases the unmarried disabled girl from the daily household responsibilities or at least lightens her burden, when both *boudi* and *nanad* work together. Sandhya remembers that once her brothers got married and her *boudis* arrived, they took over all the responsibility of the household work, leaving her to concentrate on her own work. 'After my brother got married I used to help my *boudi* with the work but stopped after a few years. Because she does the work, I don't do it anymore.' Anita says that at home she never had to do any work either for herself or for the family, as her *boudis* were all there to do whatever was needed. Moreover being disabled, none of her *boudis* ever thought of asking her to help with the work.

With authority within the family gradually devolving towards the sons and their wives, the disabled women feel powerless and sad when parents covertly support their sons, while not denying the girl her place in the family. Families, which were close and affectionate, often break into smaller households within the natal home, with brothers and their wives establishing separate kitchens.[1] Sandhya's family used to eat together after both her brothers got married until the day her *chorda* (youngest elder brother) announced that only those who work would be given food. 'Whatever I used to earn, I would give to my mother for *sansarer kharcha* (household expenses). My *dada*'s words really hurt me, as before that I never used to think much about working for money.' Rita's eldest brother and his wife have made it clear that they don't consider her to be an important part of their family. 'There was great *ashanti* (tension) at home as my *dada* and *boudi* told me that since I am a disabled girl, I should not have any scope for speaking in the family. They do not inform or consult me about family matters, as I am a disabled girl.' They used to taunt her about the food she ate, so Rita decided to support herself with her own earnings. At present, Rita's brother and his wife refuse to make her life easier by jointly renovating their home and the common pond, which would make life easier for Rita.

In Bengal, the cultural norm decrees that married sons, along with their wives, take care of the elderly parents, while daughters are married and move away from the natal home. Such ideologies accepted, internalized and valued in society sometimes varies greatly from actual practice, especially in rural areas where although living in the same household, there may be a separation of the kitchen after the marriage of sons of a family. Disabled girls who remain unmarried feel the dual pressure of such ideologies in their lives. On one hand, they feel guilty that their presence in the home may have triggered the familial turbulence; on the other, they are ashamed that their brothers willingly abdicate responsibility of their elderly parents to a disabled sister. Sandhya feels that her parents were forced to separate from her brothers because of her, because none of her married brothers wanted to assume the responsibility for their disabled sister. 'Maybe they feel that if they care for my parents, they will also have to look after me for life?' Sandhya's brothers have separated their kitchens and her parents now cook their own meals. Sandhya lives with her elder sister's family near her place of work. Sandhya took on the responsibility of supporting her parents, when her brothers refused to care for them. Sandhya has redefined the cultural expectations from daughters and feels that she can now make her own decisions as she earns her living and provides for her parents. 'I assumed responsibility for the *sansar*. I have realized *keu karor noy* (no one is your own).'

Property Inheritance

The Dayabhaga School of customary law in Bengal decrees that sons have the right to inherit property only upon the death of the father. Traditionally, landed property was passed from father to sons, which was one of the reasons for the continuation of the joint family (Urquhart 1927). Women owned no property apart from their *streedhan* (gifts received by the bride at the time of marriage), which usually consisted of wedding presents from her father and husband. It included money and jewellery, but no land. A law passed in 1956 and amended in 2005 gave daughters entitlement to a portion of the father's share of the ancestral property. However, cultural ideologies still consider daughters as having little legal right over the parental property and married daughters hesitate to claim it as they feel that their brothers are the rightful heirs. Unmarried disabled women staying in the natal home have legal rights over parental property. But unmarried daughters are seen as dependent on their brothers for maintenance and protection, and for disabled women, the notions of dependence are doubly reinforced.

Of the girls living in villages, most of their families own the land on which the home is built, while some families own agricultural land of a few *bighas* (local measure of land equal to 0.33 acre). As brothers grow up, they start helping their fathers with the agricultural work and slowly take over the major part of the responsibility from them. Within the home too, when they get married, they have separate rooms to live in, while the disabled girl shares living space with her parents, other siblings or her nephews and nieces. As disabled daughters, their claim on the natal property is judged along the lines of other married daughters, who relinquish their property rights at the time of marriage. Mothers worry about their daughter's future when they would not be around to care for her. Their greatest fear is that their disabled daughters would not be able to claim their legitimate rights. They urge their husbands to divide the property and give their daughter a share of the home property, as both accept that she will continue to live with the support of her brothers and their families. Asha's mother wants to build a separate room for her in case relations with her brother and his wife sour in future. Although Saraswati's father insists that his sons would be inheriting the property, her mother has requested him to legally register the land on which the room and bathroom for her have been built with the NGO's financial support. Girls and their parents feel that transferring agricultural land in her name would be futile as she would not be able to work on them. Sandhya clarified, 'I wouldn't be able to grow crops by myself. Nor do I have the money to hire labour. What would I do with that land?'

Fathers are reluctant to acknowledge their disabled girls as a legitimate heir to their home property and delay in taking concrete steps to ensure the inheritance of their daughter. Sulekha's father is still dithering over transferring one of their rooms in her name legally, so that she may never have to face eviction by her brother. Sandhya's father is reluctant to act on the decision of making her one of his legal heirs, even though all their relatives also have been urging him to do so. 'Many people especially my *pisi* (paternal aunt) and *jamaibabu* (elder brother-in-law) told my father to legally ensure that I inherit part of the house. But it hasn't been done yet.' Disabled girls internalize the gendered notions that decree that daughters cannot inherit, and feel ashamed to claim their share of the property, as they too believe that it should be passed on to the sons of the family. Asha insists that she will have to live with her brother and his family as long as she lives. 'What do I need a separate room for? When I die, it will be my brother's anyway.' However, as her parents are still paying off the debts incurred during her sister's marriage, Asha is expected to fund the construction of the room as she is an earning member.

As socio-cultural ideologies render disabled girls unfit to claim parental property, their disability and dependence on the natal family makes them vulnerable to ill-treatment at home from their brothers and sisters-in-law. The panchayat in Rita's village sanctioned a house for her under the Indira Awas Yojana and she has now built two rooms, one used by her mother and herself and the other by her father. When she got a loan to build a bathroom and toilet alongside the house, her elder brother, fearing that she will lay claim to the property, incited their father against her. 'My father says that he will not divide the property as long as he is alive.' Threat of defamation is commonly used to discipline, control and coerce disabled women into submission. In order to ensure that her claim to the property is weakened, Rita's brother cast aspersions on her character and behaviour. 'My *dada* tells our neighbours that I had affairs when I was working in Punjab, etc. He wants to malign my character and make it difficult for me to stay at home.' Rita feels that if she hadn't been a girl, her brother would not have found it so easy to harass her like this. 'The whole issue revolves around me, an unmarried disabled sister, and no one wants to be saddled with the responsibility for me.'

In the city, Manju has faced similar souring of relationships over property issues. Her father has passed on his business interests to his sons and also given them a share of the property in which they live. When Manju's son was born, her parents compelled her to come and live near them so that they could help care for the baby while she went to work. Her parents offered her and her husband a piece of land just opposite her natal home, where they could build their own home. Although initially reluctant, her husband finally decided to build a house on that plot. But this sparked off jealousy in her *mejdi* (second elder sister) and *chotobhai* (youngest brother), who demanded that their father gift them with similar plots of land. Gendered ideologies internalized by Manju makes her argue against her sister's actions more loudly than she protests her brother's animosity, as she feels that her sister had received a dowry much larger than hers, while her brother is represented as the 'natural' heir. Although Manju refuses to concede that it was her disability that prompted her parents to make such an offer to her, it is clear that it was because she was disabled that her parents were more concerned about her ability to manage a small baby. 'I didn't come of my own free will—my parents insisted I come here after my son was born. They felt that I wouldn't be able to manage with a little baby as I am like this.'

Relationships beyond the Natal Family

Disabled girls are apprehensive about entering into relationships with men, guided by notions of a *bhalo meye* and the imperatives of maintaining a reputation as one. Socialized into notions of femininity and desirability, with stress on physical perfection and capabilities, disabled women feel inhibited and refrain from seeking out or entertaining the attentions of men or even responding to men's overtures, fearing that they would be rejected or ill-treated. Agatha was scared to express her feelings for the man she liked as she felt that he would never contemplate any long-term commitment to her.

'I don't know why I could not reveal my feelings to him. I always felt that it would be silly of me and very stupid to do so. My disability was a very big factor in that.' Disabled girls have limited scope to interact with boys of their own age, and the men they meet are either their friends, friends of brothers, brothers of friends or colleagues at work.

Romantic Relationships

Girls with mild and moderate disabilities form relationships with men, mainly because they present a semblance of 'being complete'. For them, the process of being 'in love' is exhilarating as well as emotionally draining. For some, however, it is the ultimate rejection, which they feel, is mainly due to their impairments. Manju met 'him' at the employment exchange where she had gone to register her name after she passed the Class XII exam. They had exchanged addresses and kept in touch through letters for a few months before openly claiming a relationship. Their relationship lasted for four years, sustained through weekly meetings and letters that they wrote to each other. When Manju's family started looking for a groom for her, she broached the topic of marriage, after being prompted by her friends. 'He didn't respond at all. He started avoiding me. We would fix a meeting and he wouldn't turn up. I was devastated and broken-hearted. I never realized that he wouldn't marry me. I know he rejected me only because of my disability.'

Although the degree of disability influences social acceptability as a potential partner, class differences also act as a barrier for promising relationships. Dora met Ashok at the special school which they both attended and after years of friendship, they decided to get married. Her boyfriend, also a wheelchair user like her, now runs a computer business from his home and is self-supporting. Dora recalls their first and only date very fondly when Ashok had taken her out for a long drive in his new car and then for dinner. 'It was so romantic. I felt like a complete woman.' But Ashok's affluent parents opposed their relationship and accused Dora of trying to use him, as he was rich and successful. 'His mother told him, "If you get married to her, she might take all your money and leave you." They think I am out to grab his money. I think his mother feels that we both will be dependent on them, for money and care.' Dora believes that Ashok's parents do not want him to marry as he is also disabled and regrets that Ashok was weak and unable to resist parental pressure, which resulted in their break-up.

Girls make choices about men they like, influenced by notions of social acceptability as any other person, and are unwilling to compromise just because they are disabled. Mita's first proposal came from Mohan, a man with severe disabilities. But the social ramifications of the marriage and the gendered ideologies about husband-wife relationship prompted her decision to refuse him. 'How could I marry a man who was so severely disabled and moved by crawling? I believed that my husband would assume all responsibility for me. But I knew that if I married him, I would have to assume responsibility both for him and myself.' At the same time, Mita met Ganesh who had a mild disability at the vocational training centre and liked him. But when Mohan came to know about Ganesh, he started harassing her both at home and at the NGO where she was working in a residential position. Mohan spread rumours about Mita in her neighbourhood, and wrote suggestive letters and made abusive phone calls to her at her place of work, as a strategy to discredit her and exert pressure so that she would accept his proposal. Mita feels that Mohan wanted to destroy her reputation as a *bhalo meye* both at her home and her place of work, which is the only thing any girl needs to preserve to maintain her status in society.

Stories of Marriages

Marriages in Bengal are still largely arranged, based on selection criteria that include not only the family, lineage and caste affiliations, but also the individual merits of the prospective bride. Proposals are received either through known networks, through a *ghatak* (marriage broker) and more recently through advertisements in newspapers. Once a proposal is received, the groom's family comes to 'see' the girl and her family and judge if she will be a fit wife for their son. Usually women have very little to say about the selection of their husband, as male members of the family make the decision based on the criteria that they have set for such a selection. Marriage as an option for their future is considered only for some disabled women, who have mild impairments that is neither too visible nor affects their functional capacities. Of the five women who got married, all have mild disabilities and were considered 'marriageable' as they could perform their responsibilities, both reproductive and productive, and take charge of the her husband's *sansar*. However, three of these women got married late at around 26–28 years of age,[2] while the girls belonging to the Muslim families were married in their late teenage years. Four of the girls were given substantial dowries at the time of marriage and, of them, one has received a plot of land on which she and her husband have built a house.

These girls received proposals from a limited number of prospective grooms and some of them were revoked once the groom's family came to know about their impairment. As fathers have the responsibility of marrying their daughters, sometimes the only proposal received becomes the choice for selecting a groom for the disabled daughter. Jahanara's father was put under pressure by the unpleasant comments made by the people of her neighbourhood and community for keeping a daughter of marriageable age at home. Two years after he forced her to drop out of middle school, her father suddenly fixed her marriage to the only man who came with a proposal for her to their house. Her husband had business relations with her *mama* (mother's brother), and through him, approached her family, came to 'see' Jahanara and immediately agreed to the marriage. 'If his family had come to "see" me, then this marriage wouldn't have taken place. Who wants a disabled *bou*?'[3] Though happy with her husband, Jahanara believes that her disability was the deciding factor in her marriage especially on the part of her parents. 'My father thought that he wouldn't get any other proposal for me. Why else would he choose a dark thin man with little financial resources as my husband?' As a poor widow, Salema's mother had little option but to accept the proposal of marriage for her disabled daughter from a divorced disabled man. Yusuf, a visually challenged man from the same village, had previously married a non-disabled girl who refused to live with him and the marriage had ended in divorce after a few months. Cultural ideologies that place greater value on men decreed that Yusuf opt for a second marriage. The village people reasoned with Yusuf's father, 'A disabled girl would be a good match and they will suit each other well. If you bring a "*bhalo*" girl again, she will also leave. So bring a girl who will not dare to leave your son as she herself is disabled.'

As the onus is on fathers and brothers to ensure that the daughters of the family are married and settled with the affinal families, pressure is created on the girl to accept men chosen by their families. When Manju's *dada* declared that he would stay single to ensure that his sister would be cared for properly, she felt burdened by the decision. 'It was as if the entire responsibility was on me, for his marriage and mine too. People would tell him openly that my marriage depended on my fate. After all who would marry a girl with a defective leg?' Patriarchal bargaining operates clearly in such situations as Manju's parents started looking for a match for her only after she started earning a living, as it made her more desirable in the eyes of prospective grooms. Manju feels that men themselves are not so opposed to marrying a disabled girl, but their families are very disturbed by the fact that they are getting a flawed girl as their daughter-in-law. 'There were some men who wanted to marry me, despite my disability. Although some families agreed on hearing about the dowry my father proposed to give me, but they backed out once they knew about my disability, despite my father's promise of a good dowry.'

Although her father had explored all options for finding a suitable husband for her, Manju's marriage was finally fixed through her elder brother's business contacts. They went through a traditional process of selection of the bride, with her husband, his family members and some of his friends coming to 'see' Manju. Although initially her father-in-law had been against the marriage because of her disability, Manju's husband had insisted that he didn't have a problem with her disability. After the *ashirbad* (ritual blessing of the bride and the groom separately) of both the groom and the bride at their respective homes, the date of the marriage was also fixed. Superstitions, especially when the bride is seen to be flawed, become important in the marriage negotiations. When Manju suffered an accident about a week before the planned wedding, her father felt that it was a bad omen, and deferred the marriage giving her time to recuperate. At her husband's home also, there were discussions about the feasibility of such a marriage and her father-in-law suddenly refused to go through with the ceremony. 'He told his sons to return the advance of Rs. 5,000 which had been paid to them as part of the *pon* (dowry) and to break off the marriage.' However, her husband refused to do so and went through with the marriage despite her in-laws not attending the ceremony. Later they reconciled to the marriage.

Disabled women who chose their husbands themselves had to face a lot of opposition from different quarters, sometimes from their own family members and more often, from the family of the groom. Krishna, living in the city, met her husband while she was in college and over the years they grew close. After a few years of courtship, they decided to get married when he completed his studies. Although her family didn't have any objections, her husband's family were against the marriage. They felt that a disabled girl was unfit as wife for their son, as she might not be able to cope with the household work and might never be able to bear children. Krishna's husband was adamant. He moved out of his home and took up a job as a medical officer in a tea garden in Darjeeling. It was only then that despite strong opposition from his family they got married.

While families of the grooms usually have objections to a marriage of their son with a disabled girl because of the connotations of productive and reproductive limitations, families of women who depend on her earnings may also oppose the marriage as it means losing their financial support. Aparna faced stiff opposition to their marriage from her own mother even though she had fulfilled all her responsibilities as the oldest and the only earning member in the family. After her father died, Aparna took over his *biri* making business and supervised the workers in the village. Her husband used to make and supply *biris* to her; but when he proposed marriage, she deferred their marriage until all her sisters were married and settled. Aparna worked hard to accumulate dowry for her sisters which included money and gold jewellery as well as utensils and bedding for the household. When Aparna and her husband approached her mother about their own marriage, Aparna's mother didn't want the sole earning member to get married and leave the family. Though her husband had declined any dowry when he proposed marriage to her, Aparna had hoped that her mother would offer them some gifts or arrange for the social ceremony. Instead her mother accused Aparna's husband of breaking up their *sansar* by taking away the only earning member of the family. She tried to dissuade Aparna too, by insinuating that he wanted to marry her only for her income. Aparna was unable to understand her mother's reluctance. 'Tell me, which mother wouldn't want her daughter to get married? All mothers would be happy. Who would look after me or take responsibility for me in the future?' Aparna believes that her mother wanted only the money she brought into the family, which was used to buy gifts for her other daughters and their husbands and arrange elaborate feasts for *jamai sashti* (a ritual celebration for sons-in-law). When Aparna expressed her displeasure over this, her mother got angry and threw her out of their home. So Aparna and her husband went to her *mashi*'s (maternal aunt) house where they got married four years back.

Married Life

Marriage signifies a momentous change in lives of women, entailing responsibility for household work in a new environment as well as negotiating relationships with her newly acquired kin. For disabled women this takes on an added dimension of having to deal with ideologies that stereotype her as incapable and weak; she has to prove that she is also 'productive' and useful to their husband and his family members; she has to work twice as hard to be accepted as 'good' wives by them. The first few days of marriage is spent surrounded by extended family members, with minute interest in the way she deals with her new responsibilities and manages the *sansarer kaaj* despite her impairment. Although family members rarely comment openly on her impairment, Jahanara recalls that people in the neighbourhood referred to her as the *khoda bou* (disabled daughter-in-law). As the newest member of the household, these brides have to remain silent when the village women comment on their inability to complete all the household work in time because of their disability. The process of adjusting to a new home, milieu and family depends on the nature of the difference between the natal and the affinal home. For Salema, Aparna and Manju, who married into families living in similar circumstances as their natal family, the adjustment was not very difficult as they found means of doing things familiar. But for Jahanara, marriage meant a radical change in her living conditions and household chores. She had been used to a pucca house with toilets constructed by her father especially for her. Jahanara's new home was a mud structure with a thatched roof, having two small rooms and a small kitchen. 'The most difficult task was to learn to use open fields as a toilet as they did not have one. That was most difficult for me, considering the condition of my leg and the dark fields at night.'

While as a loved daughter with impairment, she might have enjoyed a privileged status in the natal home, marriage plunged a woman into the realm of adulthood and full responsibility. Married women are expected to be completely responsible for the *sansarer kaaj* in their affinal home, which is seen as her family and her *sansar*. Once married, women are expected to cook, wash and clean for the entire family in addition to looking after their children and also working for a living. Like others, married disabled women also have to cope with cooking for the entire family and household work like cleaning, washing clothes and utensils in their affinal family. The nature of work varies depending on whether they are living in the city or in the village. Jahanara was assigned cooking duties from the first day of her married life although her *sasuri* knew that she did not know how to cook properly. After marriage, Aparna learnt to do all the housework guided by her *sasuri,* from anointing the house walls with a mixture of cow dung and mud to fortify them, to cutting vegetables, cooking, cleaning the utensils, washing clothes, bringing water, gathering fuel from the gardens behind the house as well as making *biris* to support the family. She also mastered the skill of lighting the wooden *unan* (wood or coal stoves), managing with her 'bad' leg to fetch water for drinking and cooking from the tube well 500 m. away from their house, carrying loads of gathered firewood from the garden, etc.

Disabled women have to reconcile the material reality of their impairments to the requirements of their *sansar* and the household work they are required to perform on a daily basis. In most village homes, as fetching of water for cooking and drinking is an essential task that they have to do, married women find their own ways of dealing with it. Jahanara feels uncomfortable using the traditional *kolshi* (water pot with flat wide base and narrow neck) to bring the water, as she cannot support it on her hip properly. So she uses buckets or other such containers to carry water to her home, especially if neither her husband nor her daughters are available to help her with the task. Aparna, too, asks her husband for help if he is at home. Since most times he is hardly at home during the day, she has to manage by herself, balancing the *kolshi* carefully and walking slowly.

Kitchens are modified to the imperatives of impairment, especially in the cities, in order to allow the women to perform their role as wife to perfection. Manju who built her own house in Kolkata, modified the kitchen according to her needs, and instead of a kitchen platform, she has arranged the gas oven on the floor, with the tap close by. She has arranged the shelves in such a manner that once she sits in front of the oven, the tap, the oven and the shelves with utensils and food items are all within her reach. She prefers to sit and cook, as this allows her better control over and access to the kitchen utensils and accessories. 'If I have a heavy *kadai* (u-shaped utensil for making curry) full of curry which needs to be taken off the oven, I may lose balance and drop the whole thing if I am standing. By cooking while sitting, I can do it properly and quickly.' Women expect and receive very little help and support from their husbands who, socialized into dominant gender culture ideologies, consider helping with 'womanly' household work demeaning. Aparna's husband helps her in fetching water but only after repeated requests.

Although he does it only occasionally, she feels grateful for this small act of consideration. She covers up her discomfort by saying, 'He has his own work and has to go out also. I bring the water most of the time. When he is at home, if I am busy and request him, then he goes to bring the water. After all, he is a man. Can I expect him to go and look for himself into these things?'

Relationships with in-laws

The *natun bou* (new bride) is usually guided and helped by the other women in the family, especially the married ones like her *sasuri*, her *jaa* (co-sisters) and sometimes by her *nanad.* The *sasuri* plays a very important role in the life of her *bou.* She is the single most important person in the life of her son as well as the senior woman in the affinal family who can help the *notun bou* in adjusting to married life and responsibilities. In the initial days, it is the *sasuri* who directs the *bou* in all that she does and also helps with the performance of household work. As a *natun bou,* Jahanara was not allowed to go out of the house, and her husband, *sasuri* and *debars* (younger brother-in-law) would do all the outside work, especially fetching water, grains and other necessities from the shops. Water was brought by her husband or her *sasuri*, *debars* or *nanad.* Jahanara's *nanad*, who became her close friend, would wash all the clothes and utensils, so that she didn't have to do any heavy work around the house. Jahanara was pushed into cooking in the initial days of her marriage, but none of her in-laws ever complained about what she cooked—be it was tasteless, salty, half-cooked or over-cooked. 'My *sasuri* never scolded me or taunted me about my impairment even when I often dropped the bowl of food or burnt the food.' In those initial days, Jahanara used to find even draining water from the cooked rice a tough job because the quantity of rice cooked for the entire family was huge.

Patriarchal moral regulation and social organization ensures that women themselves engage in socializing, policing and punishing women within hierarchies of male-centred kinship structures. The husband's mother and sisters are privileged, and as the source of female power lies in husbands and sons, a woman, as mother, may command some obedience from her sons, while demanding absolute obedience from her daughter-in-law (Bannerji 2002). Krishna remembers that her *sasuri* was upset as she stayed with her parents during the whole week and with her husband's family only during the weekends. 'She kept saying to everyone, "What can you expect a *khoda bou* to do?"' Unmarried *nanads* emerge as a strong instigator of strife and violence within the family, as represented in local songs in Bengal. Aparna's only *nanad* was opposed to her marriage to her brother because she is disabled, and from the first day, tried to cause trouble between Aparna and all the other members of the family. She refused to eat any food cooked by the *khudi*, which resulted in her *sasuri* having to take over the responsibility for cooking. If Aparna sat to make *biris*, her *nanad* would taunt, 'My brother has brought home the idol of a goddess. My mother will cook and she will sit prettily in one place.' She used to hurl abuses at Aparna through the day and accused her of being oversexed. 'Why else will a disabled girl wish to get married? She has managed to trap and marry my brother.'

Husbands and wives

The husband-wife relationship is constructed as hierarchical with the wife being the *ardhangini* (half of husband's body), because in intercourse she contains part of his body. The scriptures decree passiveness, domesticity and submissiveness as qualities of a 'good' wife, whose aim in life is to please and satisfy her husband. Given away in marriage by her father's family, a woman's subjectivity and social agency is derived wholly in relation to the institutions of marriage and motherhood. For a disabled woman, the roles of wife and mother become more significant as through them, she is able to negate the connotations of incapability and incompleteness as a woman. Socialized within a cultural context that denies her sexuality and femininity, disabled women regard marriage as a means of proving their equality with all other women and strive to adhere to the roles as best as they can.

Though dominant ideology directs women to respect their husbands, disabled women elevate their husbands to the status of 'exceptional' for marrying women who are labelled as *langda* (physically disabled). 'An able man marrying a *pratibandhi meye* (disabled girl) is very rare and my husband is one of them.' Aparna is thankful to her husband for rescuing her from being tagged as *aiburo* (unmarried) all her life. When she goes to public places like the market, people remark that she is wearing *sankhapala* (bangles of red and white) and *sindoor* (vermillion), the marks of a married Bengali woman, and ask if her husband is a disabled person too. When she tells them that he is a *bhalo* (non-disabled) man, they marvel at her luck and his kindness. Disabled wives have experienced ridicule and scorn in both private and public spheres. Krishna's husband's friends used to joke with him, 'How did you manage to find a *khoda* girl to marry? He would tell them, what else could I do? It was destiny.' Aparna's *nanad* used to wonder publicly why only the *khoda* girl took his fancy, when there were so many other sisters to choose from in the same family.

The relationship between husband and wife is influenced by a number of factors, of which the rural-urban settings as well as the woman's education and financial independence are quite significant. Krishna and Manju, both from the city, educated and working, feel that their relationship with their husbands was on equal terms. Manju had made it clear to her husband and his family that she would be working after marriage. She feels that her husband had chosen to marry her because of her job and steady income, which his business was not able to offer. 'Why should a man with a steady and sizeable income marry a disabled girl? He (my husband) married a girl like me only because he was earning less.' She stressed that it was her income that increased her acceptability as a wife, despite her impairment, while her choices were limited. 'I feel girls like me, disabled women, shouldn't expect much from such relations. A normal girl can expect a lot from life but we shouldn't expect as much.'

Disabled women admit that their impairments and its material and social ramifications have affected different aspects of their married life within the family and in the larger community. They have had to seek help with some of the household tasks, especially in the rural areas, where fetching drinking water from the communal taps is a major task. When husbands help with the *sansarer kaaj* like the carrying of drinking water, women feel gratified and embarrassed. Jahanara's husband helps with all the outside work specially bringing the water for cooking and drinking purposes. Aparna feels grateful that her husband responds to her pleas of help, although he complains about having to do her share of the work. Aparna's husband grumbles that she cannot do any of the heavy work like bringing water and sometimes needs help with washing clothes and utensils. Aparna feels that her husband, being a man, has his own work and can only be asked to help when he is free. 'After all, he is a man and has to be requested for help. Men will not do it by themselves for the *sansar*.'

In the villages, within the home, gender/ability ideologies strongly influence feelings of helplessness on part of the woman, who feels her disability renders her inferior in her husband's estimation. Aparna elaborated, 'When my husband gets angry, especially when he doesn't get work or if I can't do some something properly, he taunts me for my inability.' Gendered ideologies sanction physical violence on part of men, if they are displeased with their wives. Aparna's husband beats her up regularly, egged on by his sister, and if she is unable to do something, he immediately asks, 'How did you do these things in your father's house?' Aparna regrets that her mother didn't even bother to give her the traditional gifts a bride receives from her natal home like utensils and a *kolshi* as it makes her vulnerable to taunts in her marital home. When he gets angry her husband sneers at her, 'Your *ma* gave everything to her *bhalo* daughters, but nothing to you? She celebrates *jamai sashti* with all her other sons-in-law and gives them gifts, but nothing for us? She couldn't even give you a trunk to store your things. To marry off a disabled girl like you to any other man, she would have had to give a big dowry.'

As sexuality is a very private domain, disabled women are very reluctant to talk about their sexual or physical relationships with their husbands. However, they stressed that although having sexual relations was painful and dependent on the mood of their husbands, their impairments didn't affect their capability to satisfy their husbands. Manju had been apprehensive at the beginning of her marriage, as she had been given the impression that men wouldn't prefer to engage in sexual relations with a disabled woman. In a marriage, women have very little negotiating power, especially when it comes to sexual relations with her spouse. Although Aparna doesn't enjoy the physical aspect of her marriage, her husband refuses to accept her protests. 'Even if I don't feel like it, will men listen? What is the point of saying I like that when I don't want to? Sometimes when I fight with him, he says why did you get married then? He never considers my refusal.'

In a marriage, husband-wife relations change over time and are influenced greatly by other family members. While this is a process of evolution for most couples, for Aparna, her relationship with her husband has become very bitter, because of the continuous interference by her *nanad* and *sasuri*. After the birth of their daughter, her husband had taken up a job in Kolkata and would come home only in the weekends. During the week, Aparna's *nanad* and *sasuri* gave her very little food and complained about her to her husband whenever he came home, which resulted in beatings for her every weekend. Tired of the violent behaviour, Aparna went to stay with her *mashi* (maternal aunt) who had arranged their marriage, for a few days. When she came back, her husband was not at home, but some of her neighbours told her that her husband was very angry with her. Fearing another beating, Aparna went to her mother's house where her husband sent the head of the village panchayat with a message that he wanted a divorce. At that time, Aparna was quite willing to divorce him as she 'didn't want a *ghar sansar* (home and family) anymore'. The ideology of a *bhalo meye* was once again brought into play here, with the panchayat head explaining to Aparna that a good wife would never behave in this manner, and as a disabled girl, she would not be able to manage the responsibility of her young daughter. Although Aparna came back to live with her husband due to the mediation of the panchayat head, her husband is still angry with her for seeking the help of her mother, and taunts her whenever he gets the chance. Aparna is quite disgusted with all the insults, the rude behaviour and the beatings. 'I feel that the only purpose my marriage has served is to remove my *aiburo* title, and to bless me with a child to call me *ma*.'

Motherhood

Gender ideologies in Bengal, from the time of the nationalist re-envisaging of women as mothers and the mother as the Nation, have decreed women's primary goal in life as bearing and rearing of children, as part of their *sansarik* (relating to or pertaining to the family) responsibilities. All women, single or married, are socialized to accept that a woman's duty in life is to have children in order to ensure the propagation of the husband's lineage. Giving birth to a child, especially to a male child, leads to an elevation of status, and if a woman doesn't have children, she has to lead a life of ignominy and becomes the target of sarcastic comments. For disabled women, the final means of claiming status as a 'complete' woman is by giving birth to children, thereby silencing voices that question their ability to give birth to a healthy non-disabled child. The women in Jahanara's neighbourhood started asking her a month after her marriage why she wasn't pregnant yet, and a few months later, they were speculating if she was *baja* (infertile). 'They would comment loudly in my presence about my being *baja* and my disability.' The longer a disabled married woman takes to conceive and give birth to her first child, the more the aspersions that are cast on her ability to bear and give birth to 'normal' children. The impetus to have children compels these women to seek help from different sources, ranging from divine intervention to medical doctors. Aparna went with her *sasuri* to a local Kali temple and had some medicine, which she believes helped her to become pregnant within a month of taking it.

Pregnancy doesn't result in the cessation of such comments but stimulates further discussion about her ability to give birth to a non-disabled child. When Jahanara conceived, the neighbouring women would discuss, in her presence, if the child would be born with a disability, citing examples of other disabled women who had given birth to 'normal' children. During her pregnancy, Aparna's feared about their child being born disabled were further fuelled by her *sasuri* and the other women in the neighbourhood. Salema remembers that she was very scared when she was pregnant with her first child. 'I would pray to god every day that our child shouldn't be born with a problem.' Disabled women themselves were scared of their ability to carry the baby full term, as increased weight and a shaky balance as a result of their impairment, increased the risks for them. Aparna found it very difficult to carry the weight of the baby around in the later stages of pregnancy and fell many times while fetching water or in the *ghat* beside the pond. Jahanara fell badly many times during her pregnancy and she was very scared that her child would also be born with a disability.

Pregnancy and the promise of a child made husbands more supportive and helpful towards their wives and they lent a hand with the daily household work. Manju feels that if *bhalo* girls need a lot of help during pregnancy, disabled women need more help and support during those months. As she had to go to the fields many times at night during her pregnancy for relieving herself, Jahanara's husband accompanied her every time to ensure that she did not fall and hurt herself or the baby. Manju's husband would accompany her to her office which was an hour's journey by bus from their home. In the evening, he would come to her office after work to escort her back, especially on rainy days. 'The roads near our home were really bad then and he was afraid of me falling. At that time he also helped a lot with the household work.' However, being pregnant did not preclude them from the household work as Jahanara recalls that she had to continue to cook for the entire family throughout her pregnancy, although her *sasuri* and *nanad* did help her with the chores. Although Aparna's husband and *sasuri* would help her with the heavy work like bringing water from the tubewell and gathering the firewood, she still had to manage cooking, washing her clothes and cleaning the utensils and the house.

Preconceived notions about disabled women and pregnancy influence the reactions and behaviour of people around the pregnant woman, whether they are trained doctors or neighbourhood women. When Jahanara's labour pains started the first time, her *sasuri* had gone to visit one of her *nanads*, so her husband called the neighbouring women for help. Throughout her labour, the women kept on commenting that as she was *khoda*, she didn't have the strength to push the child out. 'Being a mother about to deliver her baby, only I know how I felt hearing all those comments.' Many of the women taunted and speculated about how her husband expected a *khoda/langda* girl like her to give birth to babies. Manju and Aparna recalled being more scared after interactions with the doctors, who predicted that they wouldn't be able to have a normal delivery, and advised them to opt for a caesarean delivery as they expected that they wouldn't be able to push the baby out during labour as other women do.

Motherhood is idealized as a joy to be savoured, a proof of reaching completion as a woman. To be the mother of a son, a male heir to carry on the name and inherit property, is the main goal of all women in strong patriarchal cultures. For disabled women, their first conscious thought after the birth of their child was about the baby: although the gender of the child is important, more important to these mothers was whether the child was *bhalo.* Jahanara recalls that her first question on gaining consciousness was if the baby was disabled like her. Aparna's *sasuri* informed her joyfully that her baby was fine, perfect and non-disabled, although she was disappointed that the child was a girl. However, for Manju, the sex of the baby was as important as knowing that he was non-disabled. 'Once my son was born, everyone's fears were allayed as he was healthy, fair and male. As for me, I knew then that I wouldn't have to bear any more children.'

The birth of a child reinforces one's status as a woman and brings recognition and support from other women in the family, namely, *sasuri* and *nanads*. Jahanara recalls that her *sasuri* and *nanad* helped her in caring for all her children, from washing the *kanthas* (thin wraps made of old sarees on which the baby is lain) and bed linen, bathing them, massaging with oil, cleaning up after them and helping with the feeding. Jahanara had become very weak during the birth of her first child, and couldn't even pick up the baby for feeding. Her *sasuri* would put the baby into her arms and then take him away when he was fed and her *nanad* would rock him to sleep. Aparna's *sasuri* helped during the first few weeks after the birth of her daughter, washing all the baby's clothes, bedclothes and bed sheets and cooking for them. For Manju, her parents stepped in to help her, as she was very weak after the caesarean section. Manju went to stay with her mother, who took over the care of the newborn baby and even later as she had to join work and needed someone who could take proper care of the baby. Her mother felt that she needed extra help because she had an impairment and would not be able to manage with the child, all the housework and her job. 'My parents insisted I come and stay near them after my son was born. I was working and had a small child; who would look after the child when I was at work?'

Disabled women have found that as they grow up, their children become accustomed to having a disabled mother and learn to help her with the household chores as and when needed, especially in the rural areas. Jahanara's son and daughters bring water for her from the tap, run to the shops when necessary and also help carry utensils for her to and from the pond. Salema's eldest daughter has already learnt to light the wood oven and is now learning to make tea, so that she can help out in her father's shop. Living in the city, Manju shares a close relationship with her adolescent son and grants all her son's wishes, while her husband attempts to discipline him. Yet she feels, now that he has grown up, her son is ashamed of her disability as he tries to avoid being with her in public spaces. When they go out together, both father and son walk fast and leave her behind. 'He (my son) tells me "you walk very slowly, and I can't walk like that". So he walks fast and away from me and goes ahead. If I say that I cannot walk so fast, then my son replies "if you cannot then why come out with us?" I feel my son is now ashamed of his disabled mother.'

. The emotional journey of disabled women in their adult relationships with family members reveals their sudden entry into a painful stage, where they find themselves isolated and denied the recognition as essential members of the family, even though they contribute to family sexual division of labour and economies. Two distinct realms of relationships are noticeable, one in which the single disabled women live and experience their lives within their natal families, their married brothers and their families and with people from outside the family. The other realm is that of married women and the new relationships they forge through marriage with their *sasur-sasuri, nanad* and *debars,* their husbands and children and with the new community of which she becomes a member. In both realms, disabled women have to negotiate, compromise and adjust to new and changing situations, confront accepted ideologies and subvert existing practices.

In the natal home, disabled women grow closer to their mothers and experience a distancing of their relationship with their father and brothers. With the base of power and authority shifting from father to son, the status and recognition given to the girl within the family undergoes a re-definition and devaluation. With the coming of *boudis* into the family, disabled women find themselves being relegated to the margins, with precedence being given to the married and 'normal' woman, who is capable of assuming responsibility for the *sansar.* This woman's status in the family is affected by her financial independence and work pressures, which limit interaction between the *nanad* and the *boudi* and lessen strife, while at the same time promoting a more congenial bond based on complementarity. In families where married brothers have set up separate kitchens, women have assumed responsibility for aging parents and support them financially. Open strife between grown-up sons and disabled daughters emerges only regarding parental property, which disabled girls struggle to claim, contesting cultural ideologies that posit sons as the natural heirs.

Relations forged through marriage for women with mild and moderate disabilities entail an entire new realm where they are constantly under pressure to live up to the image of the 'ideal' woman balancing *sansarik* responsibilities along with the bearing and care of children. Like all other women, disabled women have to assume the responsibility for the entire household from day one of their married life, though they are helped by their *sasuri, nanad* and husbands at least in the initial days of marriage. Marital relations between disabled girls and their husbands are influenced significantly by her impairments, yet are negotiated on similar bases as all other women. Motherhood provides the final chance to become equal to other women as well as to improve her social status within the family and community. Although the experience of pregnancy is traumatic, more so because of their impairments, the joy of giving birth to a healthy baby and realizing the importance of being a mother prevails over all other feelings of being rejected, devalued and ridiculed as finally the disabled woman claims for herself the status of a 'complete' woman as defined by the cultural ideologies in India.

Notes

1. While in the West, a newly-married couple usually sets up an independent household, in India the practice remains of undivided families where married sons live with their wives and children in the household of their parents. With progression in time, many of these larger families are now breaking up into smaller units, sharing the same physical space but asserting independence through separate kitchen for each family unit.
2. The average age of marriage for a girl in Bengal still varies between 19 and 21 years.
3. Wife is used commonly to refer to daughter-in-law or any newly-married woman.

CHAPTER VII

Conclusion

The lives of women with disabilities in Bengal are governed by the gender ideologies that are internalized, accepted and negotiated by these women and the ways in which they carve their lives in accordance with the gender ideologies and challenge, resist or adapt them to present themselves as women. Guided by an understanding of feminist disability studies that aims to unsettle stereotypes about women with disabilities and to challenge dominant assumptions about living with a disability, it can be seen that the ways in which disabled women engage with and participate in family and social life within their communities. Although there are parallels between the ways in which social meanings are attributed to female and disabled bodies, this study unravels the cultural significance attached to the 'normal' 'perfect' female body, which by default constructs its other, the disabled female body as deviant and inferior and incapable of full participation in public as well as economic life. However, as this study brings to light, the daily lives of women with disabilities pose a challenge to cultural ideologies that construct disabled female bodies as unattractive, incapable and dependent.

The study is an exploratory one mainly because of the dearth of research in this area, especially in India, and locates the women as an integral part of and determined by the socio-cultural context in which they were born and are living. Feminist ethnography emphasizes that knowledge is contextual and interpersonal, based on women's experiences within the concrete realm of everyday reality and human agency. Employing the feminist ethnographic method enabled a deeper and meaningful understanding of the cultural context of Bengal and the gender/ability ideologies that construct, influence and impinge on lives of disabled women as well as the ways in which they challenge and negotiate the impact of such ideologies in their daily lived activities and practices. Following the feminist standpoint theory, the voices of disabled women have been given prominence in the process of describing their lives and experiences as shaped and determined by the socio-cultural context and yet resisted and redefined according to the needs of their impairments.

Of the sixteen women who participated in the study, eight have severe disability while there were four each having mild and moderate disabilities;

ages of the women varied between 24 and 40 years, with thirteen women falling in the age range of 30–40 years; ten are living in villages while six are staying in the city; only five of the mildly disabled women have been married—at present one is widowed; five of the single women are staying with their natal families, while two are staying outside the home because of their work; twelve of them are either working at present or are between jobs. Most of the women living in the rural areas belong to the poorer socio-economic group and to the lower caste groups like the Mahisyas while the women living in the city belong to the upper castes like the brahmins and kayasthas and to upper and middle class families. However, as it was difficult to locate younger and aged women with disabilities, this study represents the experiences and lives of women who are mostly middle aged.

I have illustrated the sameness of disabled and non-disabled women's experiences in their ordinary everyday lives while trying to highlight the differences which physical impairment brings into the lives of women, living in similar socio-cultural contexts of Bengal and governed by gender and ability ideologies. The gender/ability regimes that operate in the cultural context of Bengal draw heavily on the concept of the *bhalo meye*, an ideological construct of the ideal woman through representations, images, norms, practices, activities, ideas regarding acceptable bodies, appearance and behaviour, qualities and characteristics that are desirable in a girl whose destined role in life is to become a wife and a mother. The *bhalo meye* is an idealistic imaginary norm that is constructed and imbued with different qualities and expectations in different aspects of her persona and identity. Physically she must be of a particular shape and size, with a particular skin tone and features that encapsulate the cultural concept of physical beauty in a woman; in different social roles and relationships during her whole life, behaviour, comportment and qualities expected from her as well as expectations from her with respect to duties and responsibilities; culturally the concept is a repository of all the aspirations and idealizations of the Bengali patriarchal structures that project women into an exalted status as mother, comparing her to the goddess and nation, while constraining and subjugating her in the private domain and relegating her to a secondary status within the home and in society. In real life, the ideology of a *bhalo meye* is used to socialize, restrain, discipline and control all women, who are continuously measured against the ideal and found wanting in different ways.

For disabled women, the ideology of the *bhalo meye* assumes gargantuan proportions as it deems her as failing the stereotype in almost all spheres, while at the same time creating pressure on her to actualize the concept in her own life. The social construction of gender and disability in Bengal operates in multifarious ways: on the one hand, it treats disabled girls as women and confers on them ideas regarding the *bhalo meye* as guidelines that govern their entire existence; on the other hand, it renders disabled women as different and deficient, not a *bhalo meye,* by virtue of their impairments. Women speak of themselves as not being a *bhalo meye*, which doesn't mean that they are *baje meye* (bad women referring mainly to moral character) but that they are different from other *bhalo* women. The gender/ability culture in Bengal posits a conditional gendering process for disabled women, wherein specific aspects of gendered behaviour and expectations are denied to them while they are expected and forced to conform to all other aspects in the course of their private and public lives. For example feminine norms of dress, modesty and comportment is expected from them in their daily lives while their sexuality is negated and suppressed within the home and outside.

In childhood and adolescence, disabled girls find themselves being pampered and protected within their families in accordance with the Bengali cultural norms, but also experience processes of subtle differentiation, which serve to reinforce their specially different and devalued status. Ableist ideologies that construct disabled people as weak and dependent interact with gender ideologies and confront these girls in the form of discriminatory practices, that may be positive like providing extra favour and support or devaluing and negative like imposing proscriptions on participation in daily household and family activities based on assumptions of their abilities. Gender/ability ideologies represent inadequacies of the body as incapacity and inability to engage in social processes and cultural practices considered appropriate for 'normal' women. Yet within families their training to be women, in manner, behaviour and within the sexual division of labour was ensured by mothers who assigned them household tasks according to perceptions about their abilities and the material reality of their impairments. While Smita was pampered by all members of her extended family and never had to help much with the household work, Mita, though always considered by her mother as weak and dependent, had to take up the responsibility for cooking for the entire family in her teenage years, because her family had deemed her unfit to help augment the dwindling financial resources.

Girls receive messages from parents as well as teachers that gaining an education would enable them to get jobs that would pay well but would not require hard labour. Except for three women, for whom going to school was a problem, all the girls attended primary school, but many of the girls living in villages were forced to drop out as the secondary schools were physically too far for them to access. Apart from Rita who completed her secondary school living in a hostel in the city but now lives in her natal village, all the girls who have been able to access higher education are from urban centres and have used their knowledge to get 'good' jobs. However, schooling experiences reveal the individual and institutional attitudes towards disabled people and girls have had a range of devaluing encounters—from complete rejection and stigmatization like Agatha, ridicule by classmates like Mita to teachers who advised her to study as she was different from other girls like Manju. Schools as institutions reflect socio-cultural ideologies in the way in which they deal with the disabled girls—while the school in Sulekha's village refused to admit her because she was disabled and would not be able to manage within the classroom. Agatha, admitted to a premier school in Kolkata came up against discriminatory attitudes that underscored not only her difference but also her inabilities. Many of the women recall that their teachers emphasized the need for education for them especially as they were unmarriageable and needed to work to support themselves in adulthood.

In adulthood, the pampering and protection experienced by the girls in childhood changed radically as she was expected to engage in the familial sexual division of labour and is slowly marginalized because of her disability and unmarried status. Differences are created from adolescence into adulthood between 'normal' women and disabled women, highlighting their impairments and comparing it constantly to an idealistic norm in the private domain of family and household. In terms of the sexual division of labour within and outside the home, ableist ideologies represent disabled women as having reduced physical capacities and incapable of engaging in productive work. However, in the day to day lived practice, disabled women engage in and manage almost all of the activities and practices that govern daily lives of these women, although this varies according to the degree of disability. Ideologies are challenged by women who question, confront and redefine such ideas by engaging in household and other work, according to their capabilities and the demands of the families in which they are living. Many of the single women shoulder different responsibilities within the home, from cooking to cleaning utensils and washing clothes for the entire family.

While disabled women are allowed to inhabit spaces within the family and identify themselves with the women around them, their difference from other women, especially the married ones, is continuously created, maintained and reinforced in every aspect of their lives. As marriage is considered to confer full adult status on a woman, disabled women who remain single are considered to be frozen in childhood/youth, and never seen as a responsible woman of the family. This is most profoundly realized in the way disabled women are represented as engaging in *gharer kaaj* while other 'normal' women are seen to assume the responsibility for *sansarer kaaj*. As the *boudis* enter the home, they are accorded more prestige and value, as a married woman who is 'normal' and capable of assuming responsibility of the family. Work done by the disabled woman within the household, labelled *gharer kaaj*, is ideologically separated from the *sansarer kaaj* of the married women in the house, who are projected as having responsibility for the entire family and household while the disabled woman is never seen as being responsible for the *sansar.*

Gender ideologies that devalue and recognize women's work within the home and outside dismiss disabled women's efforts as inconsequential. The ideologies that represent disabled women as incapable of engaging in hard physical labour like other women also pass on dichotomous messages: while she is considered as incapable and weak and her contribution to family labour is negated, she is also made to understand that work is the only option open to her as she is unmarriageable. Disabled women work both at home and outside to contribute to the family economies, but participation varies according to need and family contexts as well as the abilities of the women. In the villages, most of the girls have responsibilities for housework and also earn a living, while only women with mild and moderate disabilities from middle and upper class families living in urban areas are responsible for such work. Financial independence was projected as a virtue for these women, who are deemed as unmarriageable by the gender/ability ideologies. However, work also emerges as something that they can actively engage in to occupy themselves, and serves to challenge ideologies that negate their worth as productive members of the family. The kind of work chosen is determined by a lot of factors, foremost being the abilities of the women, but also important were its demand within their villages, family's need for the income of the woman and her own decision to work. The degree of disability does not unduly influence participation in productive work, except for Saraswati and Chobi, as women who have grown up with impairments learn over the years to tailor the needs of their impairment to the requirements of the work they engage in. Many of the girls living in the villages work from home in various trades popular in their area like making *muri* (Sulekha), doing embroidery on sarees (Asha and Rita), part of the work in re-fashioning of garments (Salema), making *biris* (Aparna), while a few work outside the home in factories (Anita and Sandhya) or even take up agricultural work (Aparna). In the city, the women work in schools (Agatha), offices (Manju), NGOs (Mita and Krishna) and in specific income generation programmes of NGOs (Smita and Dora). However, single women with disabilities have some degree of control over expenditures, especially if they are supporting their parents.

Over the course of life, unmarried disabled girls, although living within the natal family, experience a radical change in the nature of the relationships they share with their family members. As they grow up, relationships with fathers become distanced and sometimes even hostile, especially as some fathers are reluctant to transfer part of their property in the name of their daughters. While Rita's father vehemently opposes such a move, Sandhya, Saraswati and Asha's fathers keep procrastinating the issue. Strong caring bonds are formed with mothers, who are their truest allies in the patriarchal family setup, as they are apprehensive about the future of their disabled daughters who live with their married brothers and their families. As sisters get married and move away, disabled women become lonelier as they are unable to establish the same kind of companionship with their *boudis*, who usurp their position of favour within the household just because of their marital and 'normal' status. Caring sensitive brothers get married, have children and establish separate kitchens within the home and become distanced from their disabled sister. They become wary of and antagonistic towards her presence in the natal home because of inheritance issues and an unmarried daughter's legal claims over parental property. Family politics ensures that the disabled girl becomes increasingly marginalized within the natal home and feels helpless, lonely and unhappily dependent on her brothers.

Women with mild disabilities were the only women who were considered capable of attracting proposals from prospective grooms, although gendered ideologies decree that qualities desirable in prospective brides are lacking in disabled women. Chances of marriage were also affected by class and caste considerations as well as the dowry that she is expected to receive, as it increases her value to her prospective in-laws. All the women were paid substantial dowry in keeping with their class and social contexts, even Salema who got married to a divorced disabled man. The gender/disability ideologies posit disabled men, men from poorer families or men with less education than these women, as suitable partners for them, further reinforcing the devaluation they experience. The men who marry disabled women are perceived as exceptional persons for choosing to marry a disabled woman, who needed him to wipe out the stigma of being *aiburo* all her life. Thus, a relationship deemed unequal by the gender ideologies is rendered further unequal by the ideologies regarding impairment.

Marriage catapults the girl into immediate adulthood, with responsibility for the *sansar* devolving to her as well as the maintaining of the relationships with all affinal kin. Married women engage in household work which includes cooking for the entire family, cleaning and keeping the house neat and clean, and in the villages, bringing water from the communal taps as well as scouting for fuel, managing the performance of the work in accordance with the demands of their impairments. Three of the married women are also engaged in paid work, either at home or outside, involving hard labour throughout the day while also doing all the *sansarer kaaj*. After marriage, a woman's labour is used by her husband for his and his family's benefit, and yet is devalued because she is a disabled woman. Although Aparna does all the *sansarer kaaj*, makes *biris* at home with her husband and works in the fields as a daily labourer during the agricultural season, her husband always tells her and their neighbours that she needs help for small tasks like bringing water from the village tap. There are differences, however, in perceptions and negotiations that illiterate women living in rural relatively closed communities and educated and working women in urban families engage in within their marital homes. While Manju and Krishna were on an equal footing with their husbands because both were educated and working, Salema, Jahanara and Aparna perceive themselves as dependent on their husbands and bow to their dictates, even though two of them are also earning for the family. Relationships with the in-laws are influenced by the husband-wife equations: while Aparna's in-laws behave badly with her, Manju's in-laws, who were initially against the marriage, have now accepted her within the family. For disabled women, motherhood becomes a necessity, as it is the final frontier for proving her womanhood, to gain recognition and social status within the family and community and to experience the relationship that is culturally so treasured in Bengal. After the birth of their children, women received a lot of support from their natal and affinal families in caring for the child, proving once again the loved status of a child within the family.

Feminist disability studies probes the cultural meanings attributed to bodies that societies deem as disabled and seeks to present disability as an integral part of one's embodiment, character, life and way of relating to the world (Garland-Thomson 2005). Disabled Bengali women, during their entire life course, are subjected to the same processes of gender socialization that all women living in the cultural context experience and they identify themselves primarily as women. This is in contradiction to the general labelling of these women primarily as disabled and defective, thereby negating their femininity. However, the process of embodiment for disabled women is one fraught with a series of contradictions, which they experience in adolescence and adulthood. The centrality of the body becomes evident for these women as they grow up, are subjected to and participate in gendered activities and practices within the home and outside. On the one hand, they internalize normative ideologies about a *bhalo meye*, which specifies the way in which the female body should appear and behave, as well the practices that it is allowed to engage in, within the dominant Bengali gender culture. On the other hand, disabled women are forced to accept the material reality of their impairments and deal with the requirements of their impairments while perfecting their performance as women.

Bartky (1992) and Bordo (1993) have demonstrated the different ways in which women, with and through their gendered bodies collude with, subvert and resist the norms of ideal femininity and hence sculpt their embodiment in accordance or at odds with the gendered constructions of female bodies. The experience of embodiment in their daily lives—of living with bodies deemed as imperfect, of negotiating these bodies in daily personal tasks and familial sexual division of labour, of rejoicing in and coping with pubertal processes, of participating in cultural activities in private and public domains, of enduring rejection and repression of their sexuality yet being restrained by normative directives, of marriage and motherhood—is structured by their social and material environments as well as by the kind and degree of disability. For girls with mild disabilities the adherence is total and redefinition is slight, but for girls with moderate to severe disabilities, adherence becomes more difficult, redefinition implies reviewing notions of femininity and adapting it to the needs of their impairment. So while Krishna and Rita conceal their callipers under their clothes, Sandhya who uses a tricycle, prefers to dress femininely and remains seated on her vehicle while conversing with people so as not to reveal the extent of her disability. Such measures are viewed by family and community in a paternalistic manner, where the modified behaviour is accepted on the condition that expressions of sexuality and femininity are suppressed and understated to stop any unwelcome attention from men.

The social and historical settings in which women are located affect the nature of their embodied experience as well as their articulation of it. The female body is produced not only through the cultural practices that shape and manipulate the physical body but also by the women's lived experiences of their bodies. As the constructed ideal female body is linked with social acceptability, to have an appropriate feminine body is most crucial to a woman's sense of herself as a female sexually desiring and desirable subject (Bartky 1992). Women attempt to live up to the ideologies that create and construct a feminine ideal, in terms of bodily perfection, physical capability and reproductive capacity. In everyday life, disabled women experience and negotiate their gendered/impaired bodies and lives in accordance with the socio-cultural norms of acceptable behaviour and comportment expected from women. These women internalize, accept and adhere to gendered norms, and experience impaired bodies as oppressive as their impairment interferes with their accomplishment of an appropriate feminine performance. Despite difficulties, disabled women prefer to present a semblance of feminine self to their families and in public, and choose to redefine norms according to the imperatives of their impairments. Growing up with impairment provides women with insights into negotiating them in order to adopt, adapt and tailor their performances to adhere to notions of a normative femininity.

Cultural constructions that produce the female body as desirable and attractive and capable of fulfilling both productive and reproductive functions confer on disabled female bodies ideologies of incapacity and unattractiveness in sexual and other relationships. Living in a culture where women must negotiate their identities vis-à-vis their appearance, these women engage in disciplining their own bodies through a range of every day lived practices. This process allows them to produce their own bodies according to the dictates of idealized normative construction of feminine embodiment.

Women become active producers of their bodies through internalization and pursuit of ideals of femininity propagated by cultural and media images advocating self-containment, self-monitoring and self-normalization. Women's bodies come to be tailored, by women, to conform to social ideals which are historically specific (Bartky 1992; Bordo 1995). Disabled women redefine the ideal of a *bhalo meye* in the different domains of their daily lives, whether in the private realms of their homes and personal processes or in the public spaces.

Women are given contradictory messages regarding their sexuality: while their sexuality is repressed due to ideas concerning marriageability, there are enforced proscriptions on interactions with men fearing threats to sexuality, all geared towards maintaining her status as a *bhalo meye*. Disabled girls, judged against such ideals, come to consider themselves as deficient and experience their bodies as lacking in the qualities that other female bodies possess. Rita, who reiterated during our interactions that she would have liked to get married, also revealed that she had rejected one of her male friends who wanted to marry her for fear that he would later desert her. Thus, on one hand they experience disabled bodies as oppressive as they hinder their chances of getting married and assuming a status as women and on the other hand, perceived threats from men in the public sphere reinforce the fact that though she is not a *bhalo meye*, she has to be bound by the dictates of being a *bhalo meye*. Anita, who moves about freely in her village and outside, is often made the butt of sexual innuendo and is scared that any association with men would destroy her reputation in her community as a *bhalo meye*. In urban areas, negation of sexuality is experienced in interaction with people in public where Krishna was ridiculed for dressing in a feminine manner and wearing jewellery. The process of negation and denial of the sexuality of disabled women proceeds from suppression within the household to encounters in the public sphere, that serve to reinforce the ideologies and lead to withdrawal of disabled women, sometimes reluctantly, from the arena of sexuality.

Analyses of Bengali patriarchy elaborated the ideological separation of men's and women's spheres of operation in the form of the *ghar* (home) and the *bahir* (outside world). Disabled women experience the devaluation of their bodies in *ghar* and *bahir* in different ways. Within the home, they are represented as incapable of sharing the burden of the household work or engaging in economic activity, but accepted and loved as members of their families and their inabilities are accommodated, at least within the natal family. Sandhya's sister who discounts her contributions towards the household work, worries if her sister gets late returning from work. Saraswati, who is not able to help her mother with any of the household work, is fondly reprimanded by her mother for increasing her workload. In the outside realm, disabled women are judged on the basis of appearance and constructed as incapable and unattractive, resulting in ridicule and hostility. To outsiders, the possession of impaired bodies, bodies that do not look, act or seem 'normal' becomes the main marker of their difference on which is built an entire ideological construction about the woman with disability and her abilities. Dora remembers the comments of people whenever she went out to the playground with her father. 'Why does she look like this?' or 'People like her should not be brought to the park'. Outside the home, disabled girls feel most conscious of their impaired bodies and realize their failure to live up to the expectations from female bodies. Interactions outside the home whether in neighbourhood or in the wider social spaces almost always reinforce the differences and highlight the deficiencies of the impaired feminine body.

The realization that their bodies are different from the socially constructed physical norm impels disabled women to draw as little attention as possible to themselves while they negotiate public spaces. Yet they find themselves at the centre of focus in their public encounters, with people focusing only on their impairments and ignoring their presence as women. Moreover, these stigmatizing encounters also convey messages about the ways in which disabled female bodies rouse public sympathy but are rejected and discriminated against not only because they are disabled but also because they are female. The 'gaze' constructs and devalues impaired female bodies that occupy public spaces and pushes them further into the margins of society. However, these experiences vary based on the visibility and severity of her impairment, her geospatial as well as class location, and is dependent on the girl's activities beyond the household domain. In urban areas, public spaces, which are usually unfamiliar and comprise largely of strangers, are experienced as hostile, oppressive and intolerant of the disabled girl, as is evident from the experiences of Chobi, Dora, Manju and Krishna. In rural areas, which are usually closed communities, girls experience curiosity and ideologies of devaluation from people known to them, that seek to undermine her efforts. Girls living in both urban and rural areas are more disturbed by the hostile behaviour they face in familiar spaces rather than in places where they are unknown and where anonymity helps to ward off the taunts and comments. Saraswati prefers to go to visit puja pandals in the city rather than in her village because she is not known to anyone there and the negative comments do not have the power to hurt her in comparison to those received in known contexts and in the presence of friends and family. Ridicule and taunts from people known to them increases their sense of devaluation further as they are concerned about managing situated conduct in light of normative conceptions of the community regarding attitudes and activities appropriate to one's sex/ability category.

The study has illustrated that although gender/disability ideologies construct all disabled women as unidimensional, their experiences vary significantly according to the degree of disability. Women with different kinds of disability experience their bodies and negotiate their identities in different ways as forms of resistance and the struggle for bodily control, independence and emancipation are embodied. The visual impact of the impairment, evident from modes of mobility and bodily infractions, and the functional limitations it entails determines the ways in which disability is experienced in, on and through the body. While all the women have faced creation of differences and discrimination, they have also engaged in and participated to different degrees in family and household activities. Younger women and those with milder disabilities strive more to become 'normal' as they still have hopes of being recognized as 'complete' women. For girls with severe disabilities, ideological constructions become too difficult for the girl to negate and they internalize and accept a devalued sense of self and their difference from other women. As they grow older these women become more resigned to their lives and are more accepting of their bodies and lives than the women with mild or moderate disabilities. For mildly disabled women, the struggle for attaining the status of a normal woman is more intense because of their seemingly less impairments, but the difference created is nevertheless discriminatory and stigmatizing as it is for other women. Hence, these girls, who perceive and prove themselves as capable of engaging in all activities that other women do, but yet are represented as lesser, find themselves struggling against the gender/ability ideologies throughout their lives, especially in the realm of sexuality and marriage. The private aspirations and wishes of women with disabilities constructed in accordance to gender ideologies, centre around marriage, having a *sansar* and being a mother, remain unfulfilled and are vehemently denied by single women. But they are somewhat reconciled to this fact by establishing close affective relations with nephews and nieces. For married women, although the hopes and aspirations of marriage are realized, the experience of marriage and marital relationships also brings forth the comprehension that it can be as devaluing and disempowering as remaining single, except for the cultural value placed on motherhood. The gender/disability regimes within households interact with and reflect the overarching gender/disability orders in the ways in which ideologies within families reflects the socio-cultural ideologies existing within the community.

Though disabled women, subjected to processes of differentiation, devaluation and discrimination, try to attain the semblance of normative femininity, their struggles and their resistance, however little, is clearly evident in the ways in which they redefine their performance of femininity and reconcile it to the needs of their impairments. These women, living within their families, express themselves and their agencies through the tiny changes they make in their lives by way of negotiating and presenting a feminine identity. Women make choices regarding the clothes they wear, use of mobility aids, the way they prefer to look, the way their lives are shaped through pursuit of an education or the choice of work, the small changes they effect to their home and surroundings to ensure better performance of their assigned social roles and their participation in larger social groups. From the decision to undergo surgery for a better gait (Manju) to rejecting the mobility aid which did not conform to her notions of being a woman (Sandhya) to moulding the aid to the demands of her femininity (Sulekha), women form their own opinions and enforce their decisions, regardless of the support received from their families. The manner in which they dress and the appearances they present are carefully crafted and designed to elaborate a feminine existence, despite the ideologies of asexuality that they are socialized into. Disabled women's agency can also be seen in the ways in which they pursue an education (Rita and Mita) and search for work (Sandhya and Manju) in order to give meaning to their lives, which is different from that of other women, who may not be encouraged to study or work, but are prepared for marriage and motherhood. For married women, who engage with the household work mostly by themselves, adjustments in their living conditions are effected to make life easier like Manju who has re-designed her kitchen to enable her to sit and cook and yet reach the shelves and the water tap easily. What has emerged as the most satisfying for many of the women is their participation in groups of people with similar impairments, where they are liberated by not being on show all the time and where not being able is acceptable. 'Till now I used to feel that I was in a prison. I never used to go out, never met newer people and was always restricted to one place with the same people to talk to. Now I go out once a month and meet other people, make friends. After that I have started feeling good about myself too.'

This study has also revealed the contradictory relationship between gender/ability ideologies in Bengal and the practices at the level of lived realities of the disabled women. Ideologies represent these women as weak, dependent, incapable of engaging in tasks like household work and sexual division of labour, and asexual, and influence the social construction of disabled women's bodies as lacking and deficient. The study has shown that though represented as incapable and weak, disabled women's lived realities are substantially different and their contributions to the household and family economy cannot be negated. Disabled women challenge and redefine many of these notions and ideas through the daily lived practices they engage in within their socio-cultural contexts. Like other women, disabled women experience the different possibilities and constraints in all the practices that their bodies engage in but the material reality of their impairments and the social construction of the *bhalo meye* further destabilize the process and experience of embodiment. These women experience their bodies as oppressive in the various social and cultural practices, and engage in the process of producing their bodies in accordance with the norms of femininity, while accommodating the demands of their impairments. In the process, they also redefine notions of femininity to suit their performance, while employing subversive strategies to present themselves as women. There is manipulation and strategization to construct identities of their own in the process of reconciling the socially constructed body mediated by individual agency within dominant social discourse. However, despite their struggles in their daily lives within their homes and outside, ideologies still continue to represent them as incapable and weak, ignoring the reassertions and redefining of women's roles and practices within their social and cultural contexts.

Bibliography

Abberley, Paul, 'The Concept of Oppression and the Development of a Social Theory of Disability', in *Disability Studies: Past, Present and Future*, ed. M.J. Deegan and N.A. Brooks, repr., Leeds: The Disability Press, 1987.

Abu-Habib, Lina, ed., *Gender and Disability: Women's Experiences in the Middle East*, Oxfam: Oxford, 1997.

Agarwal, Bina, 'Gender Inequality, Cooperation and Environmental Sustainability', paper written for the conference on 'Inequality, Collective Action and Environmental Sustainability', Santa Fe, New Mexico, 21–3 September 2001.

Asch, Adrienne, *Critical Race Theory, Feminism and Disability: Reflections on Social Justice and Personal Identity*, 2001, <http://moritzlaw.osu.edu/lawjournal>, accessed on 18 June 2003.

Asch, Adrienne and Michelle Fine,'Disabled Women: Sexism Without the Pedestal', in *Women and Disability: the Double Handicap*, ed. M.J. Deegan and N.A. Brooks, New Brunswick: Transaction Books, 1985.

———, 'Introduction: Beyond Pedestals', in *Women with Disabilities: Essays in Psychology, Culture and Politics*, ed. Michelle Fine and Adrienne Asch, Philadelphia: Temple University Press, 1988.

Bacquer, A. and A. Sharma, *Disability: Challenges vs Responses*, New Delhi: Concerned Action Now, 1997.

Bagchi, Jasodhara, 'Representing Nationalism: Ideology of Motherhood in Colonial Bengal', *Economic and Political Weekly*, vol. 25, nos. 42–3, 20–7 October 1990, pp. 65–71.

———, 'Socializing the Girl Child in Colonial Bengal', *Economic and Political Weekly*, vol. 28, no. 41, 9 October 1993, pp. 2214–19.

———, ed., *Indian Women: Myth and Reality*, Kolkata: Sangam Books, 1995.

Bagchi, Jasodhara, Jaba Guha and Piyali Sengupta, *Loved and Unloved: The Girl Child in the Family*, Calcutta: Stree, 1997.

Bandyopadhyay, Sekhar, 'Caste, Widow-Remarriage and the Reform of Popular Culture in Colonial Bengal', in *From the Seams of History: Essays on Indian Women*, ed. Bharati Ray, Delhi: OUP, 1995.

———, *Caste, Culture and Hegemony: Social Domination in Colonial Bengal*, New Delhi: Sage, 2004.

Bannerji, H., 'Re-generation: Mothers and Daughters in Bengal's Literary Space', in *Literature and Gender*, ed. S. Chaudhuri and Sajni Mukherjee, Hyderabad: Orient Longman, 2002.

Bartky, Sandra Lee, 'Foucault, Femininity and the Modernization of Patriarchal Power', in *Feminist Philosophies*, ed. J. Kourany, J.P. Sterba and R. Tong, New Jersey: Prentice Hall, 1992.

Begum, Nasa, 'Disabled Women and the Feminist Agenda', *Feminist Review*, vol. 40, 1992, pp. 70–84.

Bhambani, Meena, 'Societal Responses to Women with Disabilities in India', in *Women, Disability and Identity*, ed. A. Hans and A. Patri, New Delhi: Sage, 2003.

Bhattacharya, N.N., *Indian Puberty Rites*, New Delhi: Munshiram Manoharlal Publishers Pvt. Ltd., 1980.

Billimoria, R.B., *Educating the Mentally Retarded: A Study of Special Schools in Bombay*, Ph.D. thesis, Mumbai: Tata Institute of Social Sciences, 1985.

Bordo, Susan, 'Feminism, Foucault and the Politics of the Body', in *Up against Foucault: Explorations of Some Tensions between Focault and Feminism*, ed. C. Ramazanoglu, London: Routledge, 1993.

———, 'Reading the Slender Body', *Feminism and Philosophy*, ed. N. Tuana and R. Tong, Boulder: Westview Press, 1995.

———, 'Anorexia Nervosa', in *Women, Knowledge and Reality: Explorations in Feminist Philosophy*, ed. A. Garry and M. Pearsall, New York: Routledge, 1996.

Browne, Susan, Debra Connors and Nanci Browne Stern, *With the Power of Each Breath: A Disabled Women's Anthology*, Berkeley, CA: Cleis Press, 1985.

Bryson, V., *Feminist Debates: Issues of Theory and Political Practice*, London: Macmillan, 1999.

Campling, J., *Social Work with Disabled People*, Hong Kong: Macmillan, 1983.

Census of India, *Tables on Disability*, New Delhi: Registrar General and Census Commissioner, 2001, <http://www.censusindia.net/disability/disabled.html>, accessed on 19 September 2004.

Chakraborty, Sambuddha, *Andare Antare: Unnish Satake Bangali Bhadramahila*, Kolkata: Stree, 1998.

Chakraborty, U., *Condition of Bengali Women around the Second Half of 19th Century*, Calcutta: Firma KLM, 1963.

Chatterjee, Partha, 'The Nation and its Fragments: Colonial and Post Colonial Histories', in *The Partha Chatterjee Omnibus*, Delhi: OUP, 1993.

Connell, R.W., *Gender and Power*, Oxford: Polity Press, 1987.

———, *Masculinities*, Cambridge: Polity Press, 1995.

Cormack, Margaret, *The Hindu Women*, Bombay: Asia Publishing House, 1961.

Das, Veena, 'Femininity and the Orientation to the Body', in *Socialization, Education and Women: Explorations in Gender Identity*, ed. Karuna Chanana, New Delhi: Orient Longman, 1989.

Davis, Kathy, 'From Objectified Body to Embodied Subject', in *Feminist Social Psychologies*, ed. S. Wilkinson, Buckingham: Open University Press, 1996.

———, 'Embodying Theory: Beyond Modernist and Post modernist Readings of the Body', in *Embodied Practices*, ed. K. Davis, London: Sage, 1997.

Deegan, M.J. and N. Brooks, eds., *Women and Disability: The Double Handicap*, New Brunswick: Transaction Books, 1985.

Denzin, N. and Y.S. Lincoln, *Strategies of Qualitative Enquiry*, Thousand Oaks, CA: Sage, 1998.

Dube, Leela, 'On the Construction of Gender: Hindu Girls in Patrilineal India', in *Socialization, Education and Women: Explorations in Gender Identity*, ed. Karuna Chanana, New Delhi: Orient Longman, 1989.

———, *Anthropological Explorations in Gender: Intersecting Fields*, New Delhi: Sage, 2001.

Dyson, Tim and Mick Moore, 'On Kinship Structure, Female Autonomy and Demographic Behaviour in India', *Population and Development Review*, vol. 9, no. 1, 1983, pp. 35–60.

Engels, Dagmar, *Beyond Purdah? Women in Bengal 1890–1939*, Delhi: OUP, 1996.

Ferri, Beth and Noel Gregg, 'Women with Disabilities: Missing Voices', *Women's Studies International Forum*, vol. 21, no. 4, 1998, pp. 429–39.

Fine, M. and A. Asch, eds., *Women with Disabilities: Essays in Psychology, Culture and Politics*, Philadelphia: Temple University Press, 1988.

Forbes, Geraldine, *Women in Colonial India: Essays on Medicine, Politics, and History*, Delhi: Chronicle Books, 2005.

Fruzzetti, Lina M., *The Gift of a Virgin: Women, Marriage and Ritual in a Bengali Society*, Delhi: OUP, 1990.

Garland-Thomson, R., 'Feminist Disability Studies', *Signs*, vol. 30, no. 2, 2005, pp. 1557–87.

———, 'Redrawing the Boundaries of Feminist Disability Studies', *Feminist Studies*, vol. 20, no. 3, 1994, pp. 583–97.

———, *Extraordinary Bodies: Figuring Physical Disability in American Culture and Literature*, New York: Columbia University Press, 1997.

———, *Re-shaping, Re-thinking, Re-defining: Feminist Disability Studies*, Barbara Waxman Fiduccia Papers on Women and Girls with Disabilities, Washington, DC: Center for Women Policy Studies, 2001, <http://www.centerwomenpolicy.org/pubfiles/2001reshapingrethinkingredefining.pdf>, accessed on 4 July 2005.

———, 'Integrating Disability, Transforming Feminist Theory', *NWSA Journal*, vol. 14, no. 3, 2002, pp. 1–32.

Gerschick, T.J., 'Toward a Theory of Disability and Gender', *Signs*, vol. 25, no. 4, 2000, pp. 1263–7.

Gerschick, T.J. and A.S. Miller, 'Coming to Terms: Masculinity and Physical Disability', in *Men's Health and Illness: Gender, Power and the Body*, ed. D. Lobo and D. Frederick Gordon, Thousand Oaks: Sage, 1995.

———, 'Gender Identities at the Crossroads of Masculinity and Physical Disability', *Toward a New Psychology of Gender: A Reader*, ed. M.M. Gergen and S.N. Davis, New York: Routledge, 1997.

Ghai, Anita, 'Disability in the Indian Context: Postcolonial Perspectives', in *Embodying Disability Theory*, ed. M. Corker and T. Shakespeare, London: Continuum, 2002.

Ghosh, Jeeja, 'Women with Disability in India', *Integral Liberation*, vol. 6, no. 4, 2002, pp. 262–8.

Ghosh, Nandini, 'Embodied Experiences: Being Female and Disabled', *Economic and Political Weekly*, vol. 45, no. 17, April 2010, pp. 58–63.

———, '*Bhalo Meye*: Cultural Construction of Gender and Disability in Bengal', in *Disability Studies in India: Global Discourses, Local Realities*, ed. Renu Addlakha, New Delhi: Routledge, 2013.

Ghosh, Srabashi, 'Birds in a Cage: Changes in Bengali Social Life as Recorded in Autobiographies by Women', *Economic and Political Weekly*, vol. 21, no. 43, 1986, pp. Ws88–Ws96.

Gleeson, B.J., 'Disability Studies: A Historical Materialist View', *Disability and Society*, vol. 12, no. 2, 1997, pp. 179–202.

Goffman, E., *The Presentation of Self in Everyday Life*, New York: Doubleday Anchor, 1963.

Government of India, *The Persons with Disabilities (Equal Opportunities, Protection of Rights and Full Participation) Act 1995*, New Delhi: Ministry of Social Justice and Empowerment, 1996.

———, *The National Policy for Persons with Disabilities*, New Delhi: Ministry of Social Justice and Empowerment, 2006.

Hannaford, S., 'Women, Disability and Society', *Interface*, June 1989, pp. 10–12.

Harding, S., 'The Instability of the Analytical Categories of Feminist Theory', *Signs*, vol. 11, no. 4, 1986, pp. 645–64.

Hawkesworth, M., 'Confounding Gender', *Signs*, vol. 22, no. 3, 1997, pp. 649–91.

Hillyer, B., *Feminism and Disability*, Norman, OK: University of Oklahoma Press, 1993.

Hughes, B. and K. Patterson, 'The Social Model of Disability and the Disappearing Body: Towards a Sociology of Impairment', *Disability and Society*, vol. 12, no. 3, 1997, pp. 325–40.

Karlekar, Malavika, *Voices From Within: Early Personal Narratives of Bengali Women*, Delhi: OUP, 1991.

Liddle, Joanne and Rama Joshi, *Daughters of Independence: Gender, Class and Caste in India*, London: Zed Books, 1986.

Limaye, Sandhya, 'Sexuality and Women with Sensory Disabilities', in *Women, Disability and Identity*, ed. A. Hans and A. Patri, New Delhi: Sage, 2003.

Lloyd, Margaret, 'Does She Boil Eggs? Towards a Feminist Model of Disability', *Disability, Handicap and Society*, vol. 7, no. 3, 1992, pp. 207–21.

Lonsdale, S., *Women and Disability*, London: Macmillan, 1990.

Mani, D. Rama, *The Physically Handicapped in India: Policy and Programme*, New Delhi: Ashish Publishing House, 1998.

Maqbool, Salma, 'The Situation of Disabled Women in South Asia', in *Women, Disability and Identity*, ed. A. Hans and A. Patri, New Delhi: Sage, 2003.

Matthews, G.F., *Voices from the Shadow: Women with Disabilities Speak Out*, Toronto, Ontario: The Women's Educational Press, 1983.

Mazumdar, Sucheta, 'Moving Away from a Secular Vision? Women, Nation and the Cultural Construction of Hindu India', in *Identity, Politics and Women: Cultural Reassertions and Feminisms in International Perspective*, ed. V.M. Moghadam, Boulder: Westview Press, 1994.

Meekosha, H., 'Body Battles: Bodies, Gender and Disability', in *The Disability Studies Reader: Social Science Perspectives*, ed. T. Shakespeare, London: Cassell, 1998.

Meekosha, H. and L. Dowse, 'Enabling Citizenship: Gender, Disability and Citizenship in Australia', *Feminist Review*, vol. 57, 1997, pp. 49–72.

Mohit, Anuradha, 'Governance and Legislation: Initiatives of Government of India to Advance Asia & Pacific Decade of Disabled Persons', *Disability World*, vol. 2, April–May 2000.

Mohit, Anuradha and S.K. Rungta, *Regional Experiences: Legal Protection for Persons with Disabilities in India*, 2000, <http://www.interights.org/pubs/Bulletin>, accessed on 22 May 2003.

Mookerjea-Leonard, Debali, 'Jyotirmoyee Devi: Writing History, Making Citizens', *Indian Journal of Gender Studies*, vol. 12, no. 1, 2005.

Moore, H., *Feminism and Anthropology*, Cambridge: Polity Press, 1998.

Morris, J., 'Personal and Political: A Feminist Perspective on Researching Physical Disability', *Disability, Handicap and Society*, vol. 7, no. 2, 1992, pp. 157–66.

———, 'Prejudice', in *Disabling Barriers—Enabling Environments*, ed. J. Swain, V. Finkelstein, S. French and M. Oliver, London: Sage, 1993a.

———, 'Gender and Disability', in *Disabling Barriers: Enabling Environments*, ed. J. Swain, V. Finkelstein, S. French and M. Oliver, London: Sage, 1993b, <http://www.leeds.ac.uk/disability-studies/archiveuk/morris/genderanddisability.pdf>, accessed on June 2005.

———, 'Feminism, Gender and Disability', paper presented at a seminar in Sydney, 1998, <http://www.interights.org/pubs/Bulletin>, accessed on 22 June 2003.

Mukhopadhyay, C. and Susan Seymour, 'Introduction', in *Women, Education and Family Structure in India*, ed. C. Mukhopadhyay and Susan Seymour, Boulder: Westview Press, 1994.

Murshid, Ghulam, *The Reluctant Debutante: Response of Bengali Women to Modernisation 1849-1905*, Rajshahi: Rajshahi University Press, 1983.

National Centre for Promotion of Employment for Disabled People and National Association for the Blind, *The Employment Scenario in India with Reference to People with Disabilities,* New Delhi: NCPEDP-NAB, 1999, <http://www.dpa.org.sg/DPA/publication/dpipub/fall99>, accessed on 16 August 2004.

Oliver, M., *The Politics of Disablement,* Houndmills, Basingstoke: Palgrave Macmillan, 1990.

———, *Understanding Disability: From Theory to Practice*, Basingstoke: Macmillan, 1996.

Östör, Akos and Lina Fruzzetti, 'Concepts of Person: Fifteen Years Later', in *Concepts of Person: Kinship, Caste and Marriage in India*, Akos Östör, Lina Fruzetti and Steve Barnett, Cambridge: Harvard University Press, 1982.

Pandey R.S. and L. Advani, *Perspectives on Disability and Rehabilitation*, New Delhi: Vikas Publishing House, 1995.

Priestley, M., 'Introduction: The Global Context of Disability', in *Disability and the Life Course: Global Perspectives*, ed. M. Priestley, Cambridge: CUP, 2001.

Ramazanoglu, Caroline, *Feminism and the Contradiction of Oppression,* London: Routledge, 1989.

Rimassa, Paula, 'Women with Disabilities', in *The Costa Rican Women's Movement: A Reader*, ed. Abshagen Leitinger, Pittsburgh: University of Pittsburgh Press, 1997.

Roy, Manisha, *Bengali Women,* Chicago and London: University of Chicago Press, 1972.

Safilios-Rothschild, C., 'Disabled Persons' Self Definitions and their Implications for Rehabilitation', in *The Sociology of Physical Disability and Rehabilitation*, ed. Abshagen Leitinger, Pittsburgh: University of Pittsburgh Press, 1976.

Sarkar, Sumit, 'The Women's Question in Nineteenth Century Bengal', in *Women and Culture,* ed. Kumkum Sangari and Sudesh Vaid, Mumbai: RCWS, SNDT University (Mimeo), 1994.

Schriempf, Alexa, '(Re)fusing the Amputated Body: An Interactionist Bridge for Feminism and Disability', *Hypatia*, vol. 16, no. 4, 2001, pp. 53–79.

Sengupta, Shampa and Jeeja Ghosh, *Socialisation of Women with Disabilities: A View from West Bengal,* Kolkata: Actionaid India, 2003.

Shakespeare, T., 'Cultural Representation of Disabled People: Dustbins for Disavowal?', *Disability and Society*, vol. 9, no. 3, 1994, pp. 283–99.

———, 'Disability, Identity and Difference', in *Exploring the Divide,* ed. C. Barnes and G. Mercer, Leeds: The Disability Press, 1996.

———, 'The Sexual Politics of Disabled Masculinity', *Sexuality and Disability,* vol. 17, no. 1, 1999, pp. 53–64.

———, 'Social Models of Disability and Other Life Strategies', *Scandinavian Journal of Disability Research*, vol. 6, no. 1, 2004, pp. 8–21.

Shakespeare, T. and N. Watson, 'Defending the Social Model', *Disability and Society,* vol. 12, no. 2, 1997, pp. 293–300.

Sheldon, A., 'Personal and Perplexing: Feminist Disability Politics Evaluated', *Disability and Society,* vol. 14, no. 5, 1999, pp. 643–57.

Silvers, A., D. Wasserman and M. Mahowald, *Disability, Difference, Discrimination: Perspectives on Justice in Bioethics and Public Policy,* New York: Rowman & Littlefield, 1998.

Silvers, Anita, 'Disability', in *A Companion to Feminist Philosophy*, ed. A. Jaggar and I.M. Young, Oxford: Blackwell, 2000.

Skeggs, Beverly, 'Feminist Ethnography', in *Handbook of Ethnography*, ed. Paul Atkinson et al., London: Sage, 2001.

Smith, D.E., *The Everyday World As Problematic: A Feminist Sociology*, Toronto: University of Toronto Press, 1987.

Stacey, Judith, 'Can There be a Feminist Ethnography?', *Women's Studies International Forum,* vol. 11, no. 1, 1988, pp. 21–7.

Stanley, L. and S. Wise, *Breaking Out,* London: Routledge & Kegan Paul, 1982.

Stone, Sharon Dale, 'The Myth of Bodily Perfection', *Disability and Society,* vol. 10, no. 4, 1995, pp. 413–23.

Thapan, Meenakshi, ed., *Embodiment: Essays on Gender and Identity,* New Delhi: OUP, 1997.

———, 'Gender, Body and Everyday Life', *Social Scientist,* vol. 23, nos. 7–9, July–September 1995, pp. 32–58.

Tharu, Susie and K. Lalitha, *Women Writing In India: Vol. 1: 600 B.C. to Early Twentieth Century,* New York: Feminist Press, 1991.

Thomas, D., *The Experience of Handicap*, London: Methuen, 1982.

Thomas, Maya and M.J. Thomas, 'Strategies in Community Based Rehabilitation to Address Concerns of Women with Disabilities', *International Journal of Disability Studies,* vol. 1, no. 1, 2002, p. 817.

Tighe, Cynthia Ann, '"Working at Disability": A Qualitative Study of the Meaning of Health and Disability for Women with Physical Impairments', *Disability and Society*, vol. 16, no. 4, 2001, pp. 511–29.

Traustadottir, Rannveig, 'Obstacles to Equality: The Double Discrimination of Women with Disabilities', Centre on Human Policy, October 1990, <http://soeweb.syr.edu/thechp/womprt1.htm>, accessed on 14 July 2004.

Turner, Brian, *The Body and Society*, London: Sage, 1996.

Urquhart, Margaret M., *Women of Bengal: A Study of the Hindu Pardanashins of Calcutta*, Calcutta: Association Press (YMCA), 1927.

Vernon, Ayesha, 'The Dialectics of Multiple Identities and the Disabled People's Movement', *Disability and Society*, vol. 14, no. 3, 1999, pp. 385–98.

Wadley, Susan S., 'Women and the Hindu Tradition', in *Women in India: Two Perspectives*, ed. Doranne Jacobsen and Susan S. Wadley, Delhi: Manohar, 1999.

Wendell, Susan, *The Rejected Body: Feminist Philosophical Reflections on Disability*, New York: Routledge, 1996.

Whitehead, H., 'The Bow and the Burden Strap: A New Look at Institutionalized Homosexuality in Native North America', in *Sexual Meanings: The Cultural Construction of Gender and Sexuality*, ed. S. Ortner and H. Whitehead, New York: CUP, 1981.

Willis, P., *Learning to Labor*, New York: Columbia University Press, 1981.

Young, I.M., *Justice and the Politics of Difference*, Princeton: Princeton University Press, 1990a.

———, *Throwing like a Girl and Other Essays in Feminist Philosophy and Social Theory,* Bloomington and Indianapolis: Indiana University Press, 1990b.

Index